W9-CSD-829

POSSUM

and Other Receits for the
Recovery of "Southern" Being

POSSUM

and Other Receits for the Recovery of "Southern" Being

MARION MONTGOMERY

Mercer University
Lamar Memorial Lectures No. 30

The University of Georgia Press   Athens and London

Designed by Sandra Strother Hudson
Set in 11 on 12 Garamond

The paper in this book meets the guidelines for permanence and durability of the Committee on Production Guidelines for Book Longevity of the Council on Library Resources.

Printed in the United States of America
91 90 89 88 87 5 4 3 2 1

Library of Congress Cataloging in Publication Data

Montgomery, Marion.
Possum, and other receits for the recovery of "Southern" being.

(Lamar memorial lectures; no. 30)
Bibliography: p.
Includes index.
1. Southern States—Intellectual life—1865–
I. Title. II. Series.
F215.M85 1987 976′.043 86-19309
ISBN 0-8203-0926-5 (alk. paper)

British Library Cataloging in Publication Data available.

Contents

Foreword

CRAWFORD, in Oglethorpe County, is a very small, very quiet community in northeast Georgia. Marion Montgomery fits in well there. He, his wife Dot, and various combinations of children and sometimes grandchildren are very much a part of the community there in Crawford. The University of Georgia, though only a short drive away, seems far removed.

From the peace and quiet of Crawford, Montgomery has over the last twenty-five years issued a steady stream of fiction, poetry, and criticism that has established him as one of the major thinkers and writers in contemporary America. For many readers, Montgomery's promise of becoming a critic of profound influence was brilliantly realized in the volumes on Flannery O'Connor, Edgar Allen Poe, and Nathaniel Hawthorne published collectively as *The Prophetic Poet and the Popular Spirit.*

In *Possum, and Other Receits for the Recovery of "Southern" Being,* the 1986 Lamar Memorial Lectures delivered at Mercer University in Macon, Georgia, Montgomery shows again how widely he has read, how deeply he has thought, and how acutely he has perceived. Montgomery presents himself to his reader as a prophetic poet, one who sees his role as "that of calling us back to known but forgotten things." He is deliberately, avowedly Southern. But the reader may need to be forewarned that Montgomery's Southerners are a diverse group, for among them we find Alexander Solzhenitsyn, Ezra Pound, and William Carlos Williams.

Montgomery's concern, obviously, is less with place than with what he calls a "necessary 'Southernness,'" a state of mind, an attitude toward existence. He has an essentially Thomist, and Wordsworthian, attitude toward the here and now, a recognition of reality outside the perceiver, in fact an inordinate love of reality which leads to "sentiment," an engagement with the things of creation which is the source of sacramental vision.

The modern spirit—Montgomery uses the term "secular gnosticism"—is the deadly enemy of a Southernness which sees sacramentally, which recognizes the mystery in human experience, the visionary in the ordinary, just as the industrial mind, with its emphasis on the pragmatic, is the enemy of figurative language. Montgomery cites the Agrarian concern for language as crucial to the governance of relations in community. And it is ultimately to community, to the possibility of belonging, that Montgomery points if we are to recover and retain our Southernness.

In these lectures Marion Montgomery, prophetic poet, calls us back to things we have known but have forgotten. His is a valuable contribution to our understanding of the Southern spirit and of the forces in modern life which militate against it.

In her bequest establishing the Lamar Lectures, the late Eugenia Dorothy Blount Lamar wished to provide for "lectures of the highest type of scholarship which will aid in the permanent preservation of the values of Southern culture, history, and literature." This volume is an important addition to the series designed to realize that aim.

L. Kenneth Hammond
for the
Lamar Memorial Lectures Committee

Preface

IT WILL BE quickly evident that I speak as a Southerner—and quite deliberately so beyond my accidents of birth. But, as there are many Souths, there are even more discretely diverse Southerners. I must attempt, by direction and indirection, to make clear the sense in which I hold myself to be a Southerner. To do so, I must explore and clarify certain principles that have been distorted and increasingly abandoned, so that I may hope to encourage a "Southernness" which I believe vital to any community, whatever the state or country or date in history that we use to identify particular communities. My own position, though firmly anchored in an immediate local world—namely, Crawford, Georgia, in the 1980s—reaches deeper than the particulars of geography or history would suggest to most of my contemporaries. Anyone who is familiar with my writings will know, for example, that I have argued at some length for Alexander Solzhenitsyn as a "Southerner"—that I have pointed to "Southern" concerns in people as diverse as Ezra Pound in the *Cantos* and William Carlos Williams in *Paterson* as aspects of those works might be seen through the eyes of a Donald Davidson or Allen Tate. I have argued "Southern" concerns in Hawthorne no less than in Faulkner, in Henry Adams no less than in William Alexander Percy. There is a concern in the English-Welsh poet and artist David Jones, particularly in his great poem *The Anathemata,* that makes him companionable to both Allen Tate and Donald Davidson. For Jones, too, attempts through art to recover to us *anathemata,* i.e., "the blessed things."[1]

Such juxtapositions of writers and works on my part aims at a precision of meaning, rather than an abandonment of distinction, though we must remember that precision is an ideal to be worked toward. One can be *almost* precise only after great labor. My concern is to arrive at a sense of a necessary "Southernness," given our limited nature in creation, rather than to formulate a definition of "Southern" or "Southernness" suited to dictionary or textbook condensations. The direction of our concern is hinted at rather effectively by Stark Young in his essay "Not in Memoriam, but in Defense," his contribution to *I'll Take My Stand:* "we defend certain qualities not because they belong to the South, but because the South belongs to them." Those qualities are antecedent to, and fundamentally independent of, the accidents of time and place, though they most certainly are not based on principles of reality indifferent to time and place. (To clarify my choice of the word *accidents:* our particular existence in particular times and places is random since the fall from grace; our struggle is against and within those accidents toward our coming to terms with the particular time and place in which we find ourselves.) The principles I pursue are not and cannot be indifferent, not because of any limitation in the principles themselves, since those principles are inherent in creation from the beginning. Of course, they may *appear* to be indifferent, or be *made* to appear indifferent to us. Impassioned or irrational or both, we may pursue truth this side of death even into the chasm of the absurd, where all substantial being seems to vanish and leave our very consciousness a seeming illusion. That has been a major path, gradually becoming a road and then a superhighway in Western thought since the Renaissance. It is an enticing thoroughfare to casual tourists because the prospects along the way flatter consciousness with the chimera of its own power to traverse and subdue hostile country.

If I speak so deliberately as a Southerner, one may take me to understand that I speak out of our origins in English common law and out of Cicero—out of that dimension of our tradition which is still alive among us, if fitfully so. It is embedded still in the letters of our law, if less active in the spirit. That is a tradition which my good friend and fellow prophetic poet M. E. Bradford has explored forcefully and eloquently. Or one might take it that I speak in that prophetic strain of "Southernness" that unites us beyond time and place with the older Greek heroic tradition and with the Old Testament prophets. That strand, too, is in us, touched by the Anglo-Saxon tradition of the *comitatus* reflected in *Beowulf.*[2] In this tradition of the heroic, an individual becomes, by his choice and within the tradition of his fathers, a part of a larger whole than the self alone, a whole defined by custom. It is custom which helps us define the manner of our deportment toward an ordered, hierarchical world. This heroic tradition, with its strengths and weaknesses, has made vital much of this century's literature, and certainly that portion of it celebrated under the academic rubric, the "Southern Renaissance." In that literature, even when the tradition is being rejected, it is the tradition that defines the revolt.

Beyond its role in revitalizing our literature, a more general effect of that tradition has become increasingly conspicuous in the political arena. Not many will deny that our world, in the past few centuries, has seen a general shifting of principles—political, social, religious. I believe the effect of that shifting has been to disorient community, a consequence of the weakening or loss of both intellectual and spiritual integrity in individuals and in institutions. Whether one approve or oppose that shifting of principles, whose active force I shall presently characterize, it is rather obvious that a reaction to the shift has entered our national life in decisive ways. Early in the century a movement which came to be called Fundamentalism appeared; since the Korean War it has become a power to be reckoned with or against, as the past two presidential elections have shown. When one uses the term Fundamentalism one immediately thinks of a Jerry Falwell, but I should like to suggest that the spiritual stirring is wider than our limiting it to Protestant activists. The surge of popular sentimentality which made Alex Haley's *Roots* so vastly popular is a sign of a fundamentalist spirit astir. Why Haley's concern for roots should be more acceptable than, say, the concern for roots advocated by the Fugitive-Agrarians is puzzling, though in passing I offer what seems to me one curious contradiction. It is as if primitive roots, so long as they are not Northern European or Mediterranean, are the only acceptable source to the American intelligentsia, our reluctant inheritors of European tradition. Why this should be so I take to have deeper cause than the popular climate of guilt over slavery as that institution has stained our history as a nation. That is, I suspect that there is a concomitant species of fundamentalism of nineteenth-century origin now threatened by religious Fundamentalism; it lies deep in the faith of that intellectual mind that has largely dominated "respectable" thought in our country for over a hundred years. And it makes for a certain irony in the embrace of Haley's concern for roots.[3]

That concomitant species of fundamentalism, threatened as much by Haley as by the Fugitive-Agrarians I dare say, is in its immediate symptoms a mixture of Darwinian, Freudian, Marxist commitment, a religion which flourished openly so long as it was possible to maintain a faith in a mechanistic reading of life. It could do so only by ignoring or denying ontological and teleological mysteries which other "fundamentalist" concerns insist on raising, whether Haley is their spokesman or Jerry Falwell—or Jacques Maritain and E. Gilson. Too much faith has been invested, in some intellectual quarters, in a naturalistic fundamentalism, out of scientism, though it is a faith increasingly forced to give ground before not only theological and philosophical arguments, but before twentieth-century sciences as well—sciences ranging from particle physics to biology. In this respect, intellectual faith in the certainties of science, held with dogmatic, fundamental feelings, becomes more and more isolated from both science and religion.[4] Whatever one may think of Protestant Fundamentalism, as much in disarray as it appears, one thing is evident: it is stirred to activity by an intellectual presumption which has worked actively in Western history, under many aspects, one of whose primary necessities toward its own success is that spirit and mind be deracinated. Once spirit and mind are pulled out by the roots from old anchors in the reality of creation itself—in place—they are to be turned against each other as antagonists. This intellectual presumption works toward ends I consider diabolic, the restructuring—not the development—of being itself. I have spent three long volumes on the intellectual history of the attempt, but I shall not be able to avoid introducing it further in the lectures that follow.

That three-volume work is *The Prophetic Poet and the Spirit of the*

Age. And since my calling, as I understand it, is that of prophetic poet rather than that of lawyer or politician or scientist, it is in the mode of prophetic poet that I shall attempt to address you. Such a calling necessarily concerns itself with the good health not only of the individual, but of a community in time and place; and so I shall be crossing into the provinces of lawyers or politicians or theologians, perhaps even into those of educators, doctors, farmers—I trust with acceptable passport. If I do not explore English common law in our institutions or do not cite Cicero on laws or duties or the nature of a republic, I shall at least claim the mediate role in these concerns that a Homer or Virgil or Dante think proper to the poet. I have most excellent precedent nearer home as well, in that good Southerner who gave the first series of these Lamar Lectures, Donald Davidson. He, and his lifelong friend Allen Tate, found comfortable kinship with and encouragement from the great Latin poet in their own labors as poets and prophets.

Now to advance oneself as prophet is a most dangerous undertaking, as Dante makes palpably clear to us in his dramatization of a visit to the Nether World. It is important that I address the problem in advance. In Canto XX of the *Inferno,* we see the sorcerers—those who usurp God's omniscience by announcing the future in various ways. They are deep in Hell, in Circle VIII, punished for fraud by having their heads twisted backward so they can see only the past, unless they walk backward. Thus they must stumble backward toward the future of their full damnation, in Dante's metaphorically effective punishment for such presumption. Here we meet a variety of astrologers, alchemists, and prophets, including among the latter that most pitiable creature, Tiresias, whose punishment in Hell through Dante's artistry is not so great but that T. S. Eliot, in *The Waste Land,* frees him into our modern world that he may be made to suffer even more. With Dante and Eliot in mind, then, one takes up a term like prophet with caution.

I think we may be guided in our caution by a passage from St. Luke, who recounts that on one occasion Christ, "beginning at Moses and all the prophets," expounded to His followers "in all the scriptures the things concerning himself," those prophetic anticipations in ancient texts. That is, Christ certifies the Old Testament prophets. From that point in history at which, for the Christian, the timeless touches time and place and transforms history itself, there comes to be a significant distinction to be made among prophets. A Christian may not look at Tiresias or Eliot's Madam Sosostris or our Jimmy the Greek of Las Vegas in quite the same way as do those who reject that Coming which separates our measure of time into B.C. and A.D. (a separation which the Civil Liberties Union has not yet spotted). St. Thomas Aquinas addresses this new light on prophecy when he argues that the only legitimate role which I as prophet may lay claim to is that of calling us back to known but forgotten things, my attempt to recover *anathemata,* "the blessed things." In this view, I am endangered most when I presume to delve into future event with a presumption of foreknowledge.

Given the accidents of our immediate lives, we may anticipate a flood of presumptuous prophecy: we are at the edge of the calendar's turning into a new century. The very human wish increasingly stirs in the popular spirit, a wish that becomes an inclination and then a formidable desire, that all the digital registers of reality should either return to zero and a new beginning or be raised geometrically through the power said to reside in Progress. We may desire a quantum leap beyond this century's "backwardness." What will be the population of, the food supply of, the new gadgets of the coming century? There will surely be a flood of dark and bright anticipations in the years immediately ahead of us. At some danger of my own damnation, I predict a preponderance of rationalized justifications of visions of the future, as opposed to the older mystical visions anchored in the realities of human nature; that great eraser of history, passing time, has not managed quite to obliterate human fallibility in nature. No doubt the dreams of our future that I predict, whether warning of catastrophe or promising rescue, will be heavily anchored in abstractions of nature and history, with the prophet himself borrowing the robes of science rather than of poetry. That has been the tendency since the eighteenth century, abstractions of history and nature being the manipulative instruments of future programs in the name of humanity's perfection. But such secular prophecy, dependent on human intellect understood as potentially omniscient and omnipotent, must always oversimplify reality, since it reduces the mystery of contingency through a faith in an immanent, self-moving absolute than which nothing is greater—namely, man's own mind. Unmeasurable man, in one of the ironies that makes pathos the more appropriate emotional effect of modernism than comedy or tragedy, assumes the future of the world an effect of his own actions alone.

We may perhaps protect ourselves somewhat, build defenses against such absolutism, through a schoolboy parable which addresses the dangers of mind's presumptuousness in measuring complex reality. The parable comes to me from a fifth-grader and so encourages me to a confidence in the future of our young at least. A scientist, probably with a Federal grant, experimenting with a frog, first cut off one of the frog's legs and then shouted at the frog to jump. As best it could, it jumped. He repeated the experiment serially, cutting off a leg and shouting "Jump!" Each time the frog struggled, each time more desperately. When the final leg was cut off and the experimenter shouted, there was no movement. Whereupon the conclusion from the data of the experiment: if one cuts off all a frog's legs, it can no longer hear. Whether the results were published in a journal, my fifth-grader did not know. The experimenter in our parable may stand for one sort of prophet, the reductionist of being—of reality—who gets caught up in his limited measuring of being and comes at last to absurdity. My point, of course, is that we must consider whether our highly sophisticated accumulations toward conclusions, awe inspiring in their attention to complexity, may not be ultimately insufficient to embrace the complexity of existence; always, something more remains to be said. We follow Western thought about the stars from Ptolemy to Galileo to Einstein, noticing the general inclination at each point to assume it an ultimate point of knowledge, to be turned decisively upon reality. The full worth of stars, we may be sure, is yet unknown.

I shall for my part try to avoid conclusions on insufficient evidence, though even prophetic poets are first of all, as Wordsworth reminds us, men speaking to man. I shall hope to shout or whisper the right words to whatever frogs or other creatures I take up, intending to damage them as little as possible as we pursue truth rather than thesis demonstration, though I know both the inevitable difficulties and the dangers in one's own words. As I have already suggested, I shall certainly not attempt formulae conclusions addressing future encounters with contingency as if such formulae were inevitable solutions to future problems. Such must inevitably, by the very formulation, do injury to the complexity of any truth about complex reality. At the same time, I shall insist that there are some questions that must be raised, must be considered and meditated upon, and always at this present. For these are abiding questions.

As prophetic poet in these lectures, then, I shall attempt to address myself to immediate and past realities as we try to come to terms with them, to a concern with the integrity of our particularity as individuals and as community. I do so to remind us of things we have known but forgotten. The end of my concern is not prophecy about the 1990s or about the twenty-first century—about dreamed-of resolutions to contingency based on the authority of my own willed vision which forces contingency to resolution. If we come to ourselves at last in a dark wood—in *this* moment and in *this* place—perhaps we may see that the *here* and the *now* define the only circumstances in which significant action of mind or spirit is possible. To make that rediscovery is to become able at last to surrender the future through a visionary faith in our own present. It is a surrender which neither abandons the past, ignores the present, nor denies or presumes the future. That is to recover an ancient wisdom: "Sufficient unto the day is the evil thereof." Let me put my concern in the words of another prophetic poet: that poet, having desperately freed Tiresias into our dark world through a summoning of the past into the present, came to a brighter comfort in the always seemingly dark world of *now*—dark in the ominous shadow of the future. The poet says, with more cheerfulness than sometimes credited to him:

> if the Temple is to be cast down
> We must first build the Temple.

And from there he comes to a brighter comfort in the closing lines of his last considerable poem:

> We shall not cease from exploration
> And the end of all our exploring
> Will be to arrive where we started
> And know the place for the first time.

One

FIRST, CATCH A POSSUM

One of my favorite pieces of "Southern" literature is a recipe for a gourmet dish, much spoken of but little eaten. It begins: "First, catch a possum."* It doesn't dwell on the complex art of pursuit, merely directing that we should begin in the beginning, at the level of immediate reality, in the interest of the artful world to be made—in this instance long-simmered possum. I take it to be implied in the initial direction that it is an easy enough task, that anyone pretending to the art of cooking will have found possums readily to hand. The directions are quite other than those John Donne speaks in a moment of artful frustration:

Go and catch a falling star
Get with child a mandrake root
Tell me where all past years are
Or who cleft the devil's foot.

Indeed, there is anything but wry frustration in the directive, dealing as it does with the mundane rather than the esoteric. There is, however, an implicit recognition of an inclination common in humanity, the inclination to jump to ends out of an enthusiasm sparked by a momentary glimpse of the ends before engaging the necessary beginnings and middles that lead to ends. It is the inclination, for instance, that finds the housewife halfway through her cake mixing before realizing she has no vanilla extract or is two eggs short; it makes the mechanic, flat under the car with the oil pan in his face, have to call to a random spectator, "Say, buddy,

*I am aware of Mrs. Beeton's famous "First catch a hare." But possums, being more anciently upon the zoological field, are the more venerable and take precedence over hares.

could you hand me that wrench from over yonder by the vise?" In its advanced and elevated stages, at high moments of history, the inclination leaves us crying desperately, "Where is Longstreet?" But at its most generally corrosive level, where the inclination has become fitful somnambulism in the general mind, it spawns utopian hungers for easy millenarian ends. We become transported by hymns sung to the latest Great Society which is proposed as a way of avoiding the humdrum necessities of moving from and within reality—of starting at the beginning, of first catching a possum.

We tend, then, to overlook the obvious, which is why we inherit from our failed fathers such a wealth of advice. And because we do, we often value that inheritance for the wrong reasons. Epigraph is evidence that failure is universal and not our own invention. We may treasure the wisdom of our fathers in part as an indictment, hinting as such wisdom does at their own mistakes. Consider: Robert Frost is very much in favor of walls. His spokesman in that famous poem about walls, in fact, initiates the repairing of the wall, not the neighbor. "I let my neighbor know . . . and on a day we meet . . . to set the wall between us once again." The irritant to the speaker is not the inherited wisdom of the fathers, "Good fences make good neighbors," but that the present neighbor "Will not go behind his father's saying"; he holds to the saying, the letter of it, oblivious of the spirit that informs it. There is a presence in the letter speaking old failures at the level of concrete reality. Such aphorism is common history condensed for easy portage into the future and no doubt has a wealth of particularity clinging to its edges still, such detail as any novelist discovers in order to incarnate what the critic calls "theme." That is, theme is cumulative experience of reality, condensed aphorism. When tradition, bearing cumulative wisdom to us, is itself no longer valued, viable aphorism becomes merely cliché. Cliché is unacceptable not because the words are not viable but because our uses of the words have become an indifferent or uncommitted or hypocritical usage. If nothing else, Flannery O'Connor's fiction drives that point home; if we bring away from her work a single lesson, it is that if the life we save is to be our own, we'd better pay attention again to the words we say about that life.

Epigraph—cliché—I suggest is evidence that failure is universal and not our own invention, failure touching high and low matters; it is we who touch those matters through our words. "A bird in the hand is worth two in the bush." That says a great deal about failed dreams of conquests in nature, whether brought to bear upon Great Societies or upon forgotten eggs or wrenches. And because the failure touches many points at many elevations of mind and spirit, we cannot be always deadly serious in our concern with it. Forgotten eggs and a lost cavalry general affect us unequally in history's long shadow. But I suggest that we must learn, in recovering our inheritance as Southerners, the importance of the comic dimension in dealing with our failures, even in high matters. Robert Frost and Donald Davidson were compatible on the point. Indeed, Mr. Davidson's Lamar Lectures, he reports, were sparked and took a particular direction out of a playful remark his neighbor Frost made to him about a very serious event. Having praised "insubordination" as an American trait throughout a poetry reading, Frost remarked afterward to Davidson, in his "sidelong, riddling way," "You've been 'insubordinate' down there!" His reference was to a current congressional debate over "Civil Rights." But both he and Davidson understood deeper points at issue than "Civil Rights" at the popular level of that concern. Anyway, Davidson turned his own concern for insubordination into "The Thankless Muse and Her Fugitive Poets" and "The South against Leviathan," though without the playfulness that Frost, or even I, might bring to bear upon deep and high matters.

And so I am playfully serious in pointing out how far superior my "Southern" recipe for possum is to the shibboleth about birds caught and uncaught. Most conspicuously, the *counting* of birds confuses a deeper point, though from its emphasis on numbers the epigraph is conspicuously Western, almost typically American. *A* possum says an attitude quite different from that in *one* bird measured against *two*. The emphasis on quantitative value is rather post-Renaissance—a piece of folk wisdom out of history spawned by the new Northern European empirical spirit that initially rested much of its delight with the created world in summaries of square acres of a new-found continent. That spirit has come at last to the awe of existence as territory measured by light years. Sir Francis Bacon, in his *New Atlantis,* argues that the possession of facts leads to the possession of nature. "That noblest foundation that ever was upon earth," he says, meaning his utopian island of "New Atlantis" with his version of the Great Society floating thereon, has as its end "the knowledge of causes and the secret motion of things; and the enlarging of the bounds of human empire, to the effecting of all things possible." But within Bacon's vision of a New Atlantis lie some of the seed of Orwell's *1984.* We are left to consider the residual wisdom that is by-product of our history as affected by Bacon's evangelical parable in praise of the new god Empiricism and its holy spirit Progress. But let us do so without the desperate solemnness that our state in the world tempts us to. For from Bacon's "All birds are mine through knowledge—through gnosis" we seem to be faced with the conclusion in our day that "any bird whatever and wherever is better than no bird at all." Desperation must be borne with some cheerfulness.

Let us then contrast our Southern assumptions about possums to this Western or American or Northern or Yankee concern for birds in the bush. These little sluggard marsupials are inescapable, as a morning ride along our highways shows. They are constant victim but are not likely to become an endangered species, having survived the ways of the world, we are assured, since the Cretaceous period. They are old almost as that remote ancestor of Georgia pines, the gingko tree, and both the tree and the animal promise to be the only creaturely beings capable of surviving the congestions of New York or Atlanta. Possums seem to thrive on city pollution most remarkably. About once a year, you will see a picture on the front page of the *Atlanta Constitution* or *Atlanta Journal*: a possum on a window ledge of the latest high rise in New Atlanta. There will be a line or two from some green reporter expressing amazement. The tone of delighted awe is as if the camera witnesses the miracle of spontaneous generation on the twenty-third floor of an office complex. What the reporter hasn't learned yet is that the possum, like the poor, we have with us always. We have it more certainly than any rumored bird of paradise whose territory on good utopian authority is said to lie somewhere just above the reaches of the latest Empire State Building.

From the Southern point of view I am proposing, the possum makes an interesting doppelgänger, a mirror of the lowly ground in which our most presumptuous dreams remain forever anchored, preventing self-soaring beyond first principles, beyond the necessity of first catching a possum before we pursue any ambrosial recipes for the spirit. The factual description of the little creature alone is rich parable. Our first conclusion might be, for instance, that it is made by a committee rather than by nature. Nature's consort of principles at the level of reality, leading to order, proportion, clarity, unity—the actions and elements man learns of nature in that imitation of nature's actions we call community—these seem at first sight somehow missing from this particular creature. Here, in brief, is a description from a scientific account:

> *Didelphis marsupialis* (Virginia opossum): grizzled-gray, with dark eyes and black mottled ears, white face. It has 50 teeth, the only creature except toothed whales that has more than 44.

We learn also that the first digit of each black foot is clawless and opposable, like a thumb. It has a prehensile tail. It will eat anything organic and at any level of development or decay in the organic, from eggs to rank carrion, the sweep of generation in nature. One could continue with a wealth of fascinating detail, mentioning its habit of "playing possum" when threatened, mentioning also perhaps the shock to us of its face suddenly encountered at nose to nose proximity, a reflecting glass window pane interceding: like a death mask, it seems, the demonic writ small in the black eyes, narrow white face. But that is a shock of fancy, and the reality is intriguing enough, as for instance the following:

> When the new-born possum, still fetus-like, has made its dangerously difficult way along the mother's fur and into the pouch, it latches onto a teat; the teat immediately swells so that the little fellow cannot detach itself, even if it would. It is thus held fast until it has grown enough to turn loose and climb out into the world—to swing on its mother's tail.

Such details enrich our possum parable, in which we see ourselves with a shock of recognition at certain points, whether as individuals or as families in the givenness we call existence. It implies a point struck home to us in the words of an immortal possum. Walt Kelly's Pogo and friends, on an expedition against the unknown, send back a stirring message to the timid who remain safe at the heart of the Okefenokee swamps: "We have met the enemy, and he is us."[1]

But let us return to my sample of "Southern" literature, the possum recipe, since I wish presently to bring St. Thomas Aquinas to bear upon its initial injunction, "First, catch a possum." Not only is my example rich in philosophical and theological implication, as a good literary work should be, it is rich as well in empirical detail. After the injunction, it explains the preparation of this rarest of dishes—the herbs and spices needed, the baking time, all carefully ordered with the precision of those printed directions that accompany the Christmas toy one has to assemble in half-light on Christmas Eve. There is a considerable catalog of herbal impositions to be made upon the lowly flesh at hand. A buried part of the directions, we must notice, is that the possum carcass, which is to be enhanced by human art, is prepared on a basting board. It is a detail signaling that our possum artist no less than his subject is indeed "Southern." Not only is he theologian, philosopher, and scientist, but an aesthetic craftsman of words as well.

The basting board is a touch as artful as Chaucer's hidden and forgotten carpenter in the Miller's Tale. Chaucer, by titillating us with the carryings-on of Absolon and Nicholas and the carpenter's young wife, Alisoun, makes us forget the sleeping carpenter above them until Nicholas in anguish cries out "Water!" You remember or recover on your own the details necessary to our suddenly being recalled to known but forgotten things in the tale. There is a considerable chaos ensuing, to our delight and the Canterbury pilgrims' delight, all saving the Reeve. An even quieter but equally effective "hidden basting board" is planted by Flannery O'Connor in "A Good Man Is Hard to Find." In that story, a hypocritical grandmother smuggles a cat, Pitty Sing, along on a vacation trip with her family; our storyteller makes us forget the cat's presence until a crucial moment. The grandmother suddenly realizes she has led the family off the broad highway into backcountry Georgia, toward a plantation she used to know. But suddenly she recalls that plantation was actually in another state, not Georgia:

> The thought was so embarrassing that she turned red in the face and her eyes dilated and her feet jumped up, upsetting her valise in the corner. The instant the valise moved, the newspaper top she had over the basket under it rose with a snarl and Pitty Sing . . . sprang onto Bailey's shoulder.

Her son, Bailey, the driver, wrecks the car, to the delight of his children, the irritation of his wife, and the mortification (in several senses it subsequently proves) of his mother.

With these proofs of literary virtue in our possum recipe, by analogy to Chaucer's and O'Connor's art, perhaps we may put literary concern behind us for the moment and turn to the heart of this matter. After long and loving craft, after dwelling on the hours of basting, with rapt attention to the marvelously increasing beauties of kitchen odor, the perpetrator of our parable comes to its end, seemingly with the crisp and precise indifference of a Hemingway: "Take out of the oven. Throw away the possum. Eat the board." Thus is our attention returned to reality, with an appropriate shock to our romantic expectations, whether our romanticism lies in our disgust for the dish or with the shattering of our generous expectation of delight. Thus are we recalled to known but forgotten things. And in that turning is evidence of the highest requirement of good art. For what the good prophetic poet hopes to achieve through art is not the surprise of the unexpected but the shock of the expected, the most pleasing of experiences to the refined sensibility.

OUR RECIPE makes good prologue to the course in "Southern literature" we would give, aimed at the non-Southerner fascinated by our renaissance. It helps us distinguish between reality imagined—that is, reality raised by art—and caricature mistaken for reality itself by the provincial spirit, as for instance in those movie and television versions of Southern sheriffs and hillbillies and small town mayors. But even after their several decades of "you-alls" to identify *us* as outlandish, our mannerly reticence survives; we only mildly take offense at such perversions, perhaps remarking on our side such enduring words as those that say "drink you all of this." If slightly irritated, we might recall Prince Hal's words about insensitive rowdies: "I know you all, and will awhile uphold / The unyok'd humor of your idelness." The mannerly reticence is complex, a sign of community character yet surviving, if fast fading. If we do not recognize now, as once we did, the possibility that we might entertain angels unaware in the curious stranger at our door, the hint of that possibility survives so long as manners do. In addition, given the preponderance of non-Southerners as strangers, we also recognize them as the actual provincialists, especially as they exhibit provincialism as sophistication, an infectious confusion alas.[2] For we succumb to provincialism rapidly. Witness our advertising gimmicks as a substitute for friendly deportment between strangers to each other. Atlanta in particular seems bent on marketing manners, but when we advertise Southern manners, the ads become more nearly obituaries. One becomes disquieted by "friendly skies," and "Welcome South, Brother" reminds us that there is a second sense possible to such old words as "I was a stranger and you took me in." Ask some of those tourists Florida-bound through Georgia speed traps.

I suggest that a genuine mannerly reticence, through which one may serve a stranger a cup of coffee or be served by a stranger without the brash intrusiveness on either part that means indifference, is sign of a virtue to be the more treasured as it the more decays. Manners allow a warm but unintrusive recognition of personhood. But even so, we "Southerners" recognize in ourselves a fascination with spectacle that threatens our respect for personhood. That is why manners are salutary, even salvational. Perhaps we enjoy spectacle because of a residual inclination to view the moment's activities in the light of eternity. One wishes it so, though that quiet depth of interest hardly seems present when we flock to disaster. A wreck on a California freeway or Pennsylvania turnpike snarls traffic because of debris; a wreck on a Georgia road leads the traffic itself to block the road as the crowd gathers, curious to see. Our volunteer fire departments have as a major problem not putting the fire out but getting to the fire through the collected curious helpers. But it is not easy to disentangle curiosity and concern, to separate morbid-mindedness from a recognition of catastrophe in which one just might possibly prove helpful. My own guess is that our confusions in the presence of spectacle speak our gradual loss of a sense of order in community without our having equally lost a sense of responsibility. We are less certain who or whether a fire chief exists, and so may smother a fire with our bodily presence lest there be a vacuum of authority. Many a burned-out Southern family, I'm reasonably certain, knows what I'm talking about, having seen the family china wash basin and pitcher thrown out the second-story window by a concerned spectator. I'm even more certain that, within the "Southern" climate of community feeling, one still finds in the South less a fear of looting in such circumstances than of destruction through genuine concern.

There is something else couched within our manners that we might as well confess to: a playful maliciousness that I hope may not be without a certain kindness. That element is hinted at in our possum recipe in the sudden turn to conclusion, as if patience has been stretched quite far enough in the face of credulity. The uninitiated non-Southerner, we imply, not only fails to start by catching a possum but very likely ends by trying to eat it. The recipe, a shaggy possum story, aims at the general human inclination to an eager presumptuousness which a Southerner is likely to call a Northern trait. There is usually in that trait an absence of a sense of irony, to say nothing of that more important salving humor which makes possible the balanced preparation we need against a seeming randomness in creation. The Romans and such Southerners as William Alexander Percy might call it fate. Which is not to say that our "Southerner" does not recognize eager presumptuousness in himself; quite the contrary. What makes us different, we are likely to think if not say, is that we *do* recognize it in ourselves. That may be why we tend to appreciate the shaggy possum story, which to be effective has to seem probable, with the improbable present by implication up to a point where the ridiculous becomes apparent. It is as if we are prepared for the inevitably unexpected whose unexpectedness we acknowledge by irony to be our fault more than any randomness of accidental creation. It is our fault, we know in the blood, because of that very human inclination to eager presumptuousness. Thus we may brace ourselves in a range of attitudes from ironic sophistication to rowdy country humor, touching many combinations and degrees between, but always with reference to manners or the absence of manners. There is in such a range of self-recognition the temptation to maintain mannerly superiority in dealing with each other, but it is especially tempting when we must deal with those people we don't quite accept as "Southern."

The point is important and worthy of a seriousness that I shall presently manage to come to, I trust. The "Southerner" recognizes his inclination to presumptuousness; hence the romantic details for the preparation of that quintessential Southern dish, baked possum, that has been used so often by Northerners to talk about us. They usually suppose we *fry* possum. Implied in our gastral romanticism is recognition that we may be too much in love with the world, inordinately engaged by the world's body. Of course possum isn't the only possible focus for Northern ridicule of the South. There is the mint julep, cornbread and peas—one could make a list of Southern soul fare and even market much of it in foreign climes, if we call it soul food while making sure it really doesn't touch upon the questions of the soul. Not long since, soul food was indeed *the* cuisine in some Northern radical chic circles possessed by sentimentality.

What we especially react to as Southerners is presumptuousness in which there seems no recognition of possible transgression; it is this failure that is the mark of Cain on those we won't acknowledge as "Southern." And when that failure turns aggressive and overbearing, as it often does, we are likely to abandon shaggy possum stories or mannerly irony. The teeth we show are no longer that smile used to play possum; the words we say are more direct, with less of the deliberate ricochet of humor.

We Southerners have various names for those unfortunates who take accident for substance in their eagerness for the conquest of reality. One of the Fugitive poets speaks of those who are "born Yankees of the race of men." It is clear that he means to include in "Yankees" those who are given to willful, aggressive pretenses to innocence, wherever and whenever they are born. Indeed, they may be born and live all their lives in Crawford or Macon, though we may suspect a concentration of them in certain geographical districts other than the Southeast. Donald Davidson has his Robert E. Lee, in "Lee in the Mountains," refer to them as outlanders when he says of their power, ascendant after 1865, "Those people came." The understated naming has chilling effect in the poem's context, though a part of that poem's friction lies in having Lee aware that "those people" are not all from beyond the Potomac. Jefferson Davis himself is not above suspicion. Flannery O'Connor, who is more closely in sympathy with the Fugitive-Agrarians than sometimes acknowledged by her readers, speaks of "those people" in a somewhat larger context. Her terms, and mine, are modified out of Aristotle and St. Thomas. That is a distinction she has in mind in saying that southern writers traffic in the grotesque because they still recognize that which is grotesque. Insofar as one recognizes the normal—the natural—one is prepared to recognize the abnormal—the sub- or supernatural. And one of the normal, natural characteristics of human gifts is the inclination to presumptuousness. Not to recognize this common ground in us leaves us at the mercy of reality, since the failure to see turns us abnormal, makes us less human. That were indeed to be born outlandish, to be of those "born Yankees of the race of men." It is a condition suitable to alarm, but to an alarm raised to the level of our ringing the bells backward, as used to be done in Old England when the Northmen invaders were spotted. If one is Miss O'Connor, it requires that one draw large and startling pictures and shout for the almost blind and deaf. But when the outlandish dominates, when "those people" are difficult to distinguish from "we people," when aberration in community is advanced as the norm rather than discovered in random members of community, when the truly grotesque becomes accepted as the common, what then shall we do?

That such unfortunates are indeed thickly dominant is suggested by Miss O'Connor's weary Misfit in "A Good Man Is Hard to Find." Even in his own family he is a minority, "a different breed of dog" his father calls him. The Misfit must ask questions fundamental to his nature. In the story, he will not dwell at the level of appearances, of spectacle, nor does he tolerate spectacle reduced by abstraction to the level of sociology. That is, for him the complexity of existence will offer itself only to a radical engagement. Especially he is concerned with the question of evil and refuses to be turned aside by modern shibboleths, as the grandmother attempts to do. He will not credit his evil to society nor to the Establishment, nor simply to natural proclivity at the animal level. And because he will not, he is curiously appealing to many of us, not because of his particular acts of violence in the story—though we may take secret delight in what happens to Bailey, Bailey's wife, and their children. It is rather that the Misfit's violence suggests he at least is not born a Yankee of the race of men.

Let us return to Walt Kelly's Pogo, but with Donald Davidson's considerate seriousness and say that when "those people" become "we people" general alarm is justified but panic is not. It becomes imperative that we return to first things, so that we may recover both the realities of existence itself and an understanding of ourselves as limited agents within reality. We all incline to aberrant temptations: we would reconstitute existence beyond the inherent limits of being itself, whether it is our personal being or society's that we want to change, or even a more general deconstruction of nature itself. It is in connection with this inclination in us that I propose to introduce the other possum promised, the one out of St. Thomas. The little "white beast," which we have playfully explored through an imagination freed almost to the dangers of fancy, is a very concrete beast; its Indian name anchors in the sensual particulars of its existence: its face and fur and feeding habits. We have largely lost the imagistic anchor of its name. But to lose our orientation to the reality of a thing by losing its name is to turn from concrete being of the thing through careless indifference or willfulness, through slothful or eager presumptuousness. It is in this willfulness that the second possum lies curled, a deceiving creature more interior than that proposed mirror, that doppelgänger *Didelphis marsupialis.* But it is as real as that little beast in our literal swamps and cities, even though it has no immediate flesh and fur that the tongue can touch save through indirection—by words more figurative than literal. We often have to be tricked into letting it reveal itself—through irony, through humor, through such lowly entrapments as shaggy possum recipes. And so I propose one last possum story, a parable, in which the two possums may be brought together. From the juxtaposition we may gain some glimpse of that difference between the Southerner and the non-Southerner. It may well prove a difference of attitude toward the slyly hidden, seemingly unsubstantial creature which, while it affects the body of the world in direct and innumerable ways, is most difficult to catch in action in itself. So to our parable.

There was a derelict operating out of Athens, Georgia, into the surrounding countryside who supported himself—at the poverty level—by collecting beer cans for recycling. He walked the highways in the daytime, returning to Athens at night. Athens, a borrowed name whose ancient resonance has been abandoned—its advertising slogan is "Advancing Athens"; its suburbs move along its highways though not yet threatening Atlanta or Macon. One day our protagonist, in the heat of a late June, picked up what remained of one of those little white beasts. It had been much travelled upon, as John Crowe Ransom might say, by trucks and cars. It had been further rendered by the hot Georgia sun. It was as little possum as it might be and still be recognizable, having reached a level of almost absolute anonymity. It was lying on top of a bent Budweiser empty, so the derelict picked it up and sailed it across the right-of-way. With the bent can comfortably clinking against its brothers in his croker sack, he went on his chosen way. But he couldn't put out of mind the spectacle of that moment, the possum reduced to a sailing circle in the morning sun.

Now, our derelict was by history one of the remnants of the 1960s. He had fought in the old wars on college campuses, had been in and out of government buildings—local, state, and national—in under his own power, out by the power of the authorities. So despite the appearance of dereliction, he knew a thing or two about the world. For one thing, he had been born just across the county line from Athens, in Oglethorpe. After his wandering to and fro, up and down in the land, he had come back close to where he started from, back in search of his roots. But the sailing possum in the bright June sun, unfortunately, was a temptation that turned him from the path of recovery. That night, as he lay in makeshift quarters along the last railroad track into and out of Athens, he woke from troubled sleep and began to think about his epiphany with the possum remnant. By morning, he had become obsessed by a waking dream.

I must not follow him in his pursuit of the dream, leaving something to your imaginations. I say only that, knowing the power of advertising, having learned the attraction of the public media to spectacle over substance in the 1960s and beyond, he made his way to New York City. He appeared on talk shows, gave interviews to fascinated and idle reporters from the *Times* and the *Washington Post*. I have even heard that the business reporter of the *Wall Street Journal* spent hours with him. For what had happened was that he was suddenly rich, one of the Ten Young Men of the Future in one magazine's estimate. He was in control of franchise for a new fad. He had expectations of expanding into ancillary businesses—a new fast food chain, perhaps. The fad which was sweeping the country, so seriously taken as to promise even as Olympic Competition? Possum Frisbee. But the demand had become so great that he had been forced to adulterate his product, contracting for plastic possum frisbees made in Taiwan. (He remembered the pressed tin Traveller, the replica of Robert E. Lee's horse, that an uncle had bought for him at Stone Mountain. It had been stamped "Made in Japan.") There was a double problem with the Pogo Burger Chain since the shift had begun to plastic possums, though the food element was not beyond solution. The major difficulty was getting around the Walt Kelly copyright.

Now, I will not vouch for all the details in this typical American success story. I will say only that, insofar as the protagonist himself exists, he has now become an American, in spite of his origins in Oglethorpe County, Georgia. One might even conclude him the latest of the sons of Henry W. Grady; that is, if one remember Grady's "New South" speech at Christmastide in 1886, delivered at Delmonico's in New York City. Grady's speech promised terrible economic retribution upon the North by the South. That the South can out-North the North is illustrated in our parable, if we remember also that frisbees are supposed to have originated at that bastion of intellect, Yale, in the form of emptied pie plates in the hands of undergraduates after dinner. There is a certain poetic justice in this Georgia country boy's upstaging Yankees, but he could do so only because he understood our original possum recipe; the fad involves throwing a possum rather than the plate or basting board. To understand the intricate metaphor of the term *dish* was his special advantage, and he came by it, though he did not recognize its source, by being born a poor country boy in Oglethorpe County, where things are still more than they seem, so that their names too share in the resonance.

As to the story itself, it is rather Southern, even elegiac, in that it laments the protagonist as another Southerner gone wrong. He, having forsaken substance for spectacle, no longer able to recognize the difference, abuses substance in the pursuit of spectacle. The storyteller, along with Aristotle and St. Thomas, rather certainly does see the difference. The distinction is precisely where we must bring to bear upon our parable the thought of St. Thomas, who anticipates such "Southernness" gone astray. If I may once more borrow to my support that acute student of both possums and St. Thomas, Flannery O'Connor, we may say that St. Thomas recognized the grotesque when he saw it. Miss O'Connor says in her talk on "Some Aspects of the Grotesque in Southern Fiction," "I have found that anything that comes out of the South is going to be called grotesque by the Northern reader, unless it is grotesque, in which case it is going to be called realistic." That is, the non-Southerner will find our derelict walking the roadside with croker sack grotesque as he sails the first possum frisbee under the Georgia sun but conclude him reformed once he begins selling patented plastic Taiwan Possum Frisbees; now he is most realistic, a citizen it may be said of the "real" world.

Given Miss O'Connor's remark, we must not make the error of supposing that those born Yankees of the race of men are limited to Northern readers and critics of Southern fiction. The condition is more general, here and there. A member of the National Science Foundation contributed the entry for *Didelphis marsupialis,* our lowly possum, to the 1971 edition of the *Encyclopaedia Britannica.* He remarks that the creature's flesh is "enjoyed locally in the southern United States; the fur, though coarse and brittle, finds some use locally and is cheap." One has no quarrel with the factual elements of this authoritative statement. But there is a tonal quality about it that is suspect. Of course, the Fundamentalist Scientist to the contrary, scientific description cannot avoid the personal participation of the observer in the thing observed, the describer in the description, a limitation upon our participation in existence that should guard us one from another so long as we are aware of it. I speak here, not of the Heisenberg Uncertainty Principle in matters subatomic, but of an older theory: we meddle not simply in form and matter of the world but with Being itself, and in spite of ourselves. So we should not be surprised by tonal qualities in the most severely precise words. I am put on guard in this *Britannica* description by the distance of the observer from the observed—not his distance from possums in the possum pen or under the microscope but from possums on basting boards in known but forgotten kitchens. He is most probably one who has neither caught possums on October nights in company with boisterous dogs and young people, nor heard nostalgic, even sentimental, recollections of such festive occasions. It is certain that he never tasted either the flesh or the basting board. There is hint in the commentary of disdain for the provincial, though he shies just short of a sociological commentary which would mean a transgression by the biologist upon another specialist's field. The hint is in the phrase "locally in the southern United States." In *locally* and with *southern* used without its capital letter, the phrase suggests that, if one made his way to the southernmost reaches of these United States, even then he would discover possum eaten only in the suburbs—of villages perhaps. A food for the lowliest among the lowly. There is also a hint of sophisticated superiority in remarking that the fur finds "some use locally" and that presumably because it is "cheap."

I am not advocating that we organize to promote possum as the next soul food in chic New York restaurants or that Saks' feature possum stoles—unless misplaced Southern ladies in New York might be comforted by resonance in a fur piece from home. And perhaps one requires a highly refined sensibility to detect such tonal qualities in so brief a specimen of words as those I take from the National Science Foundation spokesman. But surely it is evident that, in our slide specimen of words, there is no trace of an awful wonder that possums *are,* that people *eat* possums, that *being is.* We get more of that in the green reporter's picture and puzzled words in the Atlanta papers. Nor is there any amused and bemused valuing of ingenuity or heroism in those most deprived of the deprived, those who eat and wear possum.

Since one of our concerns is to recall ourselves to literary sensibilities so that we may detect subtle tonal qualities, let us juxtapose another comment on the possum, again taken from the *Britannica.* A professor of genetics at the University of Wisconsin, in writing on the theory of evolution, says, "The opossum has seen the origin and differentiation of the orders of placental mammals from the Cretaceous." One cannot escape the celebratory in this statement, and it even seems likely that the celebrator has himself looked most immediately at this peculiar, diverse, extraordinary creature, the possum, with glowing wonder: it testifies here and now to a tradition reaching back to the dawn of motherhood in the world, to natural selection's saying "Let there be Mothers," as that first tiny remote creature latched on the first pap of the first possum mother—who came from God knows where. The only element amiss in the statement is the too-formal "o-possum," which keeps too safe a distance. One reading the sentence nevertheless knows that, given the possum's world enough and time, one could share with the Professor of Genetics some of the truly celebrative words in Josef Pieper's *In Tune with the World: A Theory of Festivity* in relation to Karl Stern's *The Flight from Woman,* through which we may discover something of why we have lost our ability to celebrate existence in the post-Renaissance world. One is therefore hesitant to dwell upon the tone as inappropriate to scientific objectivity, so welcomed is the sense of participation in being which is reflected in the tone of that brief sentence. Let us remark merely a shadow cast upon this visionary history of evolution as Revelation which has quite replaced the biblical one, by Owen Barfield's incisive little book, *Saving the Appearances: A Study in Idolatry.* One should note particularly his chapter "An Evolution of Idols."[3]

Turning from tonal evidence of impure science—of personal participation in the scientific incursion upon being—let us now engage with less whimsy that other long-promised possum. To do so may help explain why such impurities in "science" are inevitable and perhaps at the last even lead us to treasure the impurities themselves. The separate species of possum I have in mind, the one I said we must get at by the indirection of art, does not reveal itself in any biological genesis; it does not come to us with that seemingly direct inevitability of *Didelphis marsupialis* from the Cretaceous Period. However, it antedates in its origins the little white beast, going all the way back to a certain Garden and to an earlier "scientific" naming of creatures of being by the first Agrarian. By an evolutionary inheritance in our spiritual being, it is still with us, obscured by *seeming* evolution itself.

We need not attempt to recover this creature in its many manifestations since Adam; certainly I would be unable to do so with the precisions of geology's or biology's speculative history. Nor shall I attempt to speak on the several names accompanying it from pre-history on through history down to us. Let us be content to take it up in its medieval name, a name touching its very nature, as the scholastic scientist such as St. Thomas knew. This particular *possum,* my Latin lexicon rather than Linnaeus tells me, is the first person, present tense, singular form of the verb *posse.* That infinitive is the verb at the root of our words *possible, potent, potential,* and the like, words pointing toward a power resident in this most singular creature in creation, that person, the *I* or *Adam* that we are in this moment. These words having been said, one detects at once the lingering shadow of the Old Adam. It falls at the point a person detects within himself the glimmer of his own potential and so is moved to eager presumptuousness. In brief, the discovery comes as our consciousness, in relation to our will, discovers the potency of personhood, even though the *person* be restrained by heart and mind—to borrow further medieval terms that we must attach to the mystery of our peculiar possumhood.

It is this complex of particular personhood—always recognized at the particular present moment because existing in a present moment—about which St. Thomas is always and most deeply concerned, whether he is speaking or writing proofs of God's existence, or of the nature of truth, or of the nature of nature itself. And these are the very concerns that make him most "Southern," though we are more likely to recognize Southernness in versions of these concerns expressed more memorably by our poets. For instance, we recognize this Southernness in lines out of London in the 1930s concerning a suburb:

> Time present and time past
> Are both perhaps present in time future,
> And time future contained in time past.

It is such recognition that may bring us to see in bird call, in an "unheard music hidden in the shrubbery," that even the roses in that moment of personal collapse that so troubled a John Keats have "the look of flowers that are looked at" beyond the looking that any Adam, any particular person—Adam or St. Thomas or Keats or Eliot—is capable of giving. In a more "Southern" mode, "To the Lacedaemonians," Allen Tate speaks to those "born Yankees of the race of men." He recalls us to known but forgotten things that are in St. Thomas and Eliot:

> When I was a boy, the light upon the hills
> Was there because I could see it, not because
> Some special gift of God had put it there.

There stirs the *possum* of our present pursuit, the "I am able" within which Cain is also potential.

Out of this "Southernness" which Tate speaks of, St. Thomas is led to address most carefully—most rigorously through intellect and most passionately through his instinctive love of creation—the multitude of questions concerning the discrete person's existence tence and that person's relation to other existences once he has said *possum*—"I am able." For we must not overlook the great heart in St. Thomas which is obscured to us by his towering intellect. He is the great medieval scientist, but as such he understands the head's *scientia* as properly limited by its complement the heart, lest one become perversely gnostic through eager presumptuousness. For him, the head is restrained and must ultimately be limited by heart. As Aquinas puts the point in *Questiones disputate de veritate,* his treatise on the pursuit of truth, "Although the knowledge which is most characteristic of the human soul occurs in the mode of the *ratio,* nevertheless there is in it a sort of participation in the simple knowledge which is proper to higher beings, of whom it is therefore said that they possess the faculty of spiritual vision."

This latter faculty St. Thomas understands as one shared with the angelic order. It is the faculty of nondiscursive vision, the one experienced by the poet or mathematician which we are likely to call intuition or insight, whose active operation in us we call the imagination. In the moment at which fragments of knowledge possessed by the *ratio* coalesce in a larger meaning—"click" in relation to each other, as we are apt to say—we exclaim "I see" (*video*) or "Eureka," (I have found it). That is the visionary moment, a discovery of the expected; a return, as it were, to known but forgotten things. And it is the heart's faculty that orients the visionary so that he does not, at least for the moment, suppose himself the cause of that which he has found or which he at last sees. Thus that moment of emotional confusion when the poet has found metaphor or the scientist a growth in a culture dish on the windowsill that prophesies penicillin. *Confusion*: it is a nuclear moment, a *con-fusion,* which we cannot maintain, though its fallout continues upon the spirit long after. That is the moment of simplicity beyond division which gives us most dangerously the sense and feeling that we have participated in divinity.

I have said we must get at this oldest *possum,* this "I am able," by indirection; we have come upon the reason for that necessity here. It is through that inherited creature in us, I suggest, that we are prevented direction. It makes all compasses go awry. *I am able* becomes dominant. Lost is its complement, *I am enabled,* with its implication of agency separate from the "I," the present Adam. We must un-fuse the visionary moment, separate its constituents, in order to articulate the experience, to regain ordinate composure.

There must in consequence be forever an incommensurate distance between our witness to the vision and the vision itself. Still, as St. Thomas reminds us, we must not ignore as operative that intuitive intellect (which the scholastics speak of as *intellectus* as differing from the *ratio*), for it alone makes rational seeing ordinate. It is the vestigial heart that gives that tone of wonder in our scientist's remark that the possum "has seen the origin and differentiation of the orders of placental mammals from the Cretaceous." The tone here moves the strict scientific diction beyond the merely measured.

The disparity between the witness and his vision, between the moment of *con-fusion* and his falling away into the burden of bearing witness to the moment, troubles one. And properly so, whether he is melancholy Keats waking from the visionary moment of the nightingale as though in that waking moment he had drunk of some dull opiate; or perhaps he is that more cautious Keatsean James Joyce, with his concern for a precise management by the *ratio* through words ordered to control his "epiphanies." The disparity between vision and its witness which is not to be surmounted seems to be best addressed by the prophetic poet; he bears witness to mystery in the present. We need but think of St. John of the Cross or of St. Augustine. The language necessary to adequacy is beyond the reaches of logic; the rational, discursive intellect is insufficient, even though that is the most characteristic mode of knowledge. That is why the fanatics of a strict rationality tend to be baffled by mystical witness, by what can only seem a stuttering sequence of vague hints of some signal experience of being. For their part, the poets are as likely to react excessively to the dogma of terms chiseled by the *ratio,* arguing that, through such terms, being itself is reduced to formulae. That action Wordsworth says is one whereby we "murder to dissect." Little wonder we must concern ourselves with C. P. Snow's "Two Cultures," with Eliot's dissociation of sensibility; for we have lost that good "Southern" understanding of the complementary roles of thought and feeling, the soul's complementary modes of heart and head. But the dissociation is not so recent, of course, as the time of Milton and Dryden or the emerging triumph of nineteenth-century gnosis. By indirection, I have hinted it as ancient as Adam's being required to name the creatures in an old Garden.

The visionary moment to poet or scientist has in it implications too easily overlooked, too often deliberately ignored by both poet and scientist. But to ignore the recovery of a concert between heart and head at the *con-fused* moment of vision is just the failure that allows the particular *possum*—man always anciently present, in this present moment—to presume he is sole agent in his self-vision; his "I am able" rises to an assumption that his own potency is itself the first cause of what he sees. Through his vision, he becomes his own visionary god. That is the distortion that leads to the antithesis of Self and Other, a perversion of ordinate "ableness," concerning which Andrew Lytle makes a good medieval, Thomistic observation: "The opposite of love," says Mr. Lytle, "is not hate, but power."

Mr. Lytle's words we recognize and credit at once as "Southern," I trust. The statement is pertinent as theme to much of what has come to be acknowledged as "Southern" literature, and especially pertinent to most of the greatest of that literature. As instances, consider Mr. Lytle's own *Velvet Horn,* Robert Penn Warren's *All the King's Men,* Flannery O'Connor's *The Violent Bear It Away,* Faulkner's *Absalom! Absalom!* It is certainly a theme that possessed me in my own *Fugitive* and *The Wandering of Desire.* And since the recognition of the old *possum* is conspicuous in our writing, let us turn to those concerns more locally taken, in those provinces spoken of as the "southern United States" in the *Britannica* comment. But I urge that we do so in the light of that good "Southerner," St. Thomas Aquinas. What we shall want to consider is the particular nature of man, mankind's peculiar gifts of being, as understood intuitively by the prophetic poet; that is, as understood through the heart, in whose support the head must always be summoned. For art, says St. Thomas, is reason in making. Let us consider those gifts with which man is blessed that lead him to name himself *possum*—to say as an act of knowing his own being, "I am able," whence flows the history of the world which we are always troubled to consider if we are to know this present moment, the moment in which each of us is always saying, each in his own fashion, "I am able."

THE ARTIST, in the light of St. Thomas (which is to say, in the light of a recovery of that concert between the artist's heart and head in the presence of immediate creation), accepts his call as a maker, knowing that, because created in the image of God, he is inescapably a maker. Each of us *makes,* in accordance with the peculiar, particularized, limited gifts through which we divine and refine our personhood. It is a principle of our being which we deduce by the head's reasoning and the heart's understanding, both those actions stirred out of faith. For the artist, this means he is called to imitate, not nature, but the creative activity of nature. That is to say, he does not hold a mirror up to creation, as the historian attempts to do, but concerns himself with the probable or possible. Nor does he, by contriving a hall of mirrors, distort nature in an abuse of art whose end is some gnostic restructuring of the world, though repeatedly that has been ideologies' uses of art in our century.

What the artist discovers in the practice of his art is what any particular person discovers in the pious practice of the gifts of his calling, the gifts of his enabling. As an agent in nature, one brings a potential being toward some perfection of its potential. We speak here of the potential being of a story or poem or of a garden or building under construction. But, miracle of miracles, whatever task of making falls under our particular guidance, the stewardship we exercise in making our "thing" helps realize reciprocally a potential within our own being. In writing the good poem, our being is changed, even as the being of the reader of a good poem may be enlarged or fulfilled, a point Rilke celebrates in his "Bust of Apollo" when he says to its viewer, "You must change your life." Such development in our being is not likely to result, however, when our primary attention is on our own good. For the poet's attention should be centered in an interest in the good of the thing made; that is to say, when our commitment is that of love, as opposed to self-love. The mystery here is that through an unself-reflective love, the self is loved into a larger being, by indirection as it were. That is one of the themes abroad in *Job* or *Oedipus Rex,* a theme counterpointed in Marlowe's *Doctor Faustus* or Goethe's *Faust.* Again, by the very stewardship of that which is not ourselves, with which we exercise our gifts in the world, we grow reciprocally. In perfecting our gifts by exercising them with piety, which word is not automatically translated "solemn" or "straight-faced," we *become.* At the level of nature, then, we are "made" by our labor.

We have come to recognize the lesson in a partial, limited way recently to a degree that invites comic response from a "Southern" perspective, at least toward some instances. I have in mind the semireligious devotion among us to jogging, aerobics, body-building through diet, and the like. If the general threat of war and pestilence abroad in the world has been great prompter to religious conversion among us through the ages, the recent shadows of cancer and heart disease have a similar effect upon us individually; we come to fear most excruciatingly for that little world of man, our own private bodies. The comic response is prompted when the anxious concern is limited to a conception of life reduced to the biological. When there are religious, even evangelical, overtones among body builders as they contemplate fibers in their diet, the piety toward the self seems distorted. Such confusion of ends is one of the mischievous points involved in Miss O'Connor's story "The Life You Save May Be Your Own." The highway safety slogan itself, in the interest of the common weal, the community, rather implies community a conglomerate of well-functioning bodies. Both Socrates and Dante would be baffled by this reduction of so rich a mystery as life.

Whether we speak of either effect—of the artist's struggle to make a thing beyond himself or of his struggle to become the gifted person—the effect is flawed when the artist ignores or forgets a fundamental point: the given is presupposed. That is the first possum to catch if we are to keep control of that subtle and potentially destructive *possum.* "I am able," we repeat, means at least "I am enabled." Concerning our givenness: first is the gift of being itself; that which underlies all creation and so grounds all particulars in creation; that which the scholastics speak of as *esse,* the root of the *sum* in our *possum.* Existence, then, is the active ground in creation, that which precedes any possibility of asserting "*I* exist," which in turn is a visionary moment just preceding our assertion "I am able." All of these acts of recognition are sequential to my act of writing the pentameter line or setting narrative in motion, whether or not I am conscious of having moved through that sequence from givens.

Creation, let us say, is the infinite sum of particularity whose active ground is being itself. If I am right in making such a summary, then creation must include the person—the artist and gardener and editor and lawyer and teacher—no less than poems and gardens and office buildings and editorials and briefs and lesson plans, to speak nothing at the moment of trees and stones and rivers, or of our ubiquitous Virginia possum. I think this recognition of such importance that I dwell on it. For through our understanding of this crucial point we may be able to make our long way back into that personhood which is our true inheritance and thereby move toward a viable community of persons. It is only at this most elementary level of recovery that we shall be able to reclaim that integrity of personhood which makes this little world we refer to as "I" larger than toned muscles and organs to be saved from highway carnage. In consequence of such restoration, order may at last return in the general accommodation of families to community.[4]

But how are we to get from *esse* to *possum*? That is the abiding question. How to discover the relation of particular being to the active ground of being from which existence de-pends, of one Marion Montgomery to *beingness* itself? Gilson speaks of the problem in his little book *The Spirit of Thomism:* "actual existence, which Thomas calls *esse* is that by virtue of which a thing, which he calls *res* [an *instance* of what we call above the sum of particularity, the totality of creation], is a being, an *ens* [in short, a Marion Montgomery]."[5] The point is far more esoteric in statement than in our inescapable experience of its actuality. It is the point absolutely crucial to us if we are to understand a sacramental vision we each are witness to from time to time, as poet or scientist or any other possum catcher. And since words are the chief aid we have, since we lack as primary to our being the full angelic mode of intuition, we must always come to words, to signs. As Eliot's ribald protagonist in *Sweeney Agonistes* says, "I gotta use words when I talk to you." Now, the moment of sacramental vision I mean is the one that occurs when we engage any *thing* of creation beyond ourselves and find ourselves lifted into a confused moment, after which moment of confusion we return to what we are likely to call the mundane. We have already introduced this concern when we spoke of the *con-fusion* of the visionary moment. We will have experienced, at least for that moment, a stirring of the soul. I am sure you can recall instances of such moments, and certainly our literature abounds with memorials to them—spots of time, Wordsworth calls them; still points, Eliot calls them.

One of the most readily available literary instances, since even in our world of academic decay it remains a standard in elementary literature courses, I have already introduced: John Keats's "Ode to a Nightingale." We need not explicate the poem at length to call attention to an aspect of it usually overlooked. The visionary moment which the poem addresses has already passed for the speaker before his words begin; the speaker is falling away from that moment, though the poem is an active, heroic struggle to recover that moment. The struggle fails as heroic struggles usually do, but with such an artful dramatization of our common experience that the poem is one of the great artifacts we may pass on to our heirs in creation. You will remember the opening lines:

> My heart aches, and a drowsy numbness pains
> My sense, as though of hemlock I had drunk,
> Or emptied some dull opiate to the drains
> One minute past, and Lethe-wards had sunk.

Since the moment is passed and the speaker awakening into the mundane, he finds that world more deeply haunted by death precisely because of a timeless moment which his thought now suggests was merely an illusion, a moment which head cannot recover though heart ache toward recovery. The transcendent moment seems now so deeply stained by time, by thought's conclusion of entrapment under dark trees and within a darkness embalming the speaker through his senses—despite flickering light and the smell of flower essence in the air—that the speaker feels doomed by time. He fears that the visionary moment was only that of a waking dream, and so he tends to mistrust the heart's message to the head. Still the speaker is left wondering whether the present moment of thought in the body and in nature is the illusion or whether the moment of transport was. Do I wake now to reality, or am I asleep in the body's reality? And so the poem comes to a disturbed stasis. Of all the questions we ask of our being, this is the most persistent. The voice in the final lines drops toward silence, but the agony continues unabated.

There is a more hopeful engagement of the visionary moment in a work which helped Mr. Eliot escape precisely Keats's entrapment, a work of seminal virtue to *The Waste Land,* namely St. Augustine's *Confessions;* the Keatsean episode we have already alluded to is "The Vision at Ostia" (Book IX). The passage casts considerable light upon any of Keats's odes, as it does on the crucial section of Eliot's "Ash-Wednesday," Section III, the poem in which Eliot dramatizes an escape from Keats's closed world. Eliot's Section III begins:

> At the first turning of the second stair
> I turned and saw below
> The same shape twisted on the banister
> Under the vapour in the fetid air
> Struggling with the devil of the stairs who wears
> The deceitful face of hope and of despair.

It is in this section that Eliot gives us at last a view, from a balcony in England rather than from a balcony at Ostia; we witness a reconciliation of the body of the world to the cause of that body, and the speaker through his experience finds his senses returned to the pursuit of spirit without rejecting the body. The broad-backed sexual god Priapus is in the foreground, beyond which one sees a lady going in St. Mary's colors. I am fond of suggesting that from this moment on in Eliot's poetry, his concrete imagery no longer carries the uncomfortable queasiness about the sensual which one finds in his earlier poetry. Yet the imagery of his later poetry is quite often very much that of the earlier. But he has returned to the place from which he started, the sensuous world, and begins to see that place for the first time, no longer able to set it aside in the manner of the Manichaean. He has come to see, that is, that one approaches God, the Cause of the sensual world, first through the senses, as St. Thomas teaches.

Instead of pursuing St. Augustine and Keats and Eliot as they ask crucial questions about that "Southernness" which is the special quarry we would catch (this recognition of and acceptance of existence, with the awful consequences of its givenness), I prefer to introduce a local instance of the moment's vision. That way we will have evidence that "Southernness" is still alive in the South itself, which is not always evident; we will I trust see something of its universality even though it be given such local incarnation. Let us look briefly at Flannery O'Connor's *The Violent Bear It Away.* We know that Miss O'Connor knew St. Augustine and St. Thomas and Keats and Eliot and many, many others whose concern is the visionary moment. But let us not forget also how well she knew the immediate sensual world with its variety of inhabitants, the particularity of central Georgia. In her novel both the unlettered Tarwater and the pseudo-lettered Rayber experience Keatsean moments and flee in terror as long as they can. But they do so out of an immediate encounter with the concrete world, not through philosophers or poets.

The novel dramatizes the flight from that essential "Southernness" that concerns us. Both Tarwater and Rayber react in terror against a mystery at the heart of an immediate givenness, the world to which our senses bring us. They fear to be caught up in what Eliot calls "the still point at the center of the turning world." Tarwater is haunted by his inclination to a mysterious country in which he fears he may encounter moments of arrest, but his most disturbing discovery is that the country he fears lies in the very heart of the ordinary world of touch and taste and smell and seeing. The novel engages, as its principal antagonist to its characters, the mysterious Presence in the everyday; the clear Thomistic point is that it is only man's bored, indifferent seeing of the world through the senses that keeps him from encounter with that Presence. O'Connor's characters, strangely grotesque and distorted to so many of her readers, are her heroes precisely because they are unable or refuse to deny at last the always present threat of mystery in creation itself. Insofar as they are unable to deny the threat, they tend toward pathos, as does Rayber; insofar as they refuse, they tend toward the heroic, as does young Tarwater—and as also does the Misfit, we might add. In these violent characters, violence itself is an acknowledgment that establishes a ground in which reconciliation to being and to the Cause of being becomes possible. Miss O'Connor remarks, in defense of her Misfit, that she prefers to think that "However unlikely it may seem, the old lady's gesture [which precipitates his shooting her], like the mustard-seed, will grow to be a great crow-filled tree in the Misfit's heart, and will be enough of a pain to him there to turn him into the prophet he was meant to become. But that's another story." That other story, for our purposes, is her second novel, and her Misfit is young Tarwater.

If St. Thomas is right about our senses allowing our first movement toward God, toward that country Rayber and Tarwater in their separate ways resist, then the only final escape of that pulling or calling of the senses to existing things is to negate the existing world, the world of our senses, by gnostic thought. But short of the death of the body, that attempt is doomed. We remember that Haze Motes in *Wise Blood* fails in his attempt. I think no Southern writer places a higher value upon the world's body than Flannery O'Connor, and those critics who persist in charging that she hates the world are not to be trusted. They confuse Miss O'Connor with her characters like Rayber, an error barely tolerable in freshmen beginners. For the one sure presence in her fiction is the belief that we are inexorably pulled toward God by the simple exercise of our sensual natures, whether or not we recognize or accept that "Calling" that is in things perceived. It is grace, everywhere threatening us through the sensual world, that is her principal antagonist.

Young Tarwater, the central character, fights desperately to keep the ordinary merely ordinary, lest he be forced to give himself to that "hideous vision" he has from time to time of himself "sitting forever with his great-uncle [Old Tarwater], staring at a broken fish and a multiplied loaf." He at first takes his immediate uncle, Rayber, and his view of existence as the road to freedom. His resistance to the prophetic vision of Heaven here is evidence of the Huck Finn in him (as it is in all of us)—a tendency to reject beatitude with the wily help of St. Thomas's *possum* become rampant in our spirit: I myself am able to take care of my own affairs. Or, as Tarwater would have it, let God tend to his own "bidnis"—and the Devil as well. The more one is bored with creation, the more tempted to restructure it to exclude not only the Heaven of the preachers and philosophers and prophets and poets, but in the final extremity of revolt to exclude the world itself. (Of course, there is some reason to sympathize with Huck as he tries to deal with the widow's vision of Heaven, even as there is reason for irritation in young Stephen Dedalus's indifference as artist to both the created world and his created world of art.)

But what threatens Tarwater more terrifyingly than his distorted version of Heaven as a perpetual slavering over the multiplied loaves and fishes is the ordinary visionary moment in which a thing in nature is seen in itself, seen to the depths of its givenness. That is the depth Gerard Manley Hopkins celebrates as the "inscape" of things. Young Tarwater fears that the hunger he sees in his great-uncle may be his also by inheritance; he fears that his hunger "might be hidden in the blood and might strike some day." And so, given the fear, he tries to anchor himself in the world, at the sensual level of the world; thereby he may escape such wild spiritual temptations as he thinks he sees in old man Tarwater. But as we know from our faith in St. Thomas's argument, it is precisely the level of the senses that opens the most direct road to the spiritual, and that is what Tarwater is forced to deal with. "It was as if he were afraid that if he let his eyes rest for an instant longer than was needed to place something—a spade, a hoe, the mule's hindquarters before his plow, the red furrow under him [Miss O'Connor's tribute to Hopkins's visionary "Windhover"?]—that the thing would suddenly stand before him, strange and terrifying, demanding that he name it and name it justly and be judged for the name he gave it. He did all he could to avoid this threatened intimacy of creation." For the reality that justifies Tarwater's terror is that no thing existing can be absolutely anonymous, can be nameless, because each thing has a maker. That indeed would seem to be the thematic point of Adam's exercise of naming in the Garden. Nor may the ritual of naming be understood as arbitrary, as the Nominalist would have it, except by a willful distortion of reality itself through denying the givenness of creation.

We each experience this "threatening intimacy of creation" from time to time, and it is to be hoped that we all seek it from time to time as well. It is the underlying excuse for a considerable national industry associated with vacations at the beach or in the mountains. Those substitutes for formal retreats, of course, are as often strategy to avoid encounter with the world as attempts to regain it, as the multitude of camping gadgets for at-home convenience in the wild-wood suggests. Increasingly it is difficult for us to get away for a few days, as we say, without feeling it obligatory to take along a television set of some sort. Now the attempt to escape the threat of creation's intimacy led to the emergence of a specialized literature in Europe in the nineteenth century, in which the threat in things was dramatized as diabolical. Thus the literature of the grotesque made an imaginative adaptation of that ancient Manichaeanism which rejects creation.[6] One of Miss O'Connor's interests through her art is to turn the Manichaean use of the grotesque against itself. She often brings that literary tradition from the continent into conjunction with eighteenth-century rationalism, as in the poignant struggle in Rayber.

Rayber, a pseudorationalist, tries to come to terms with what his reason can explain only as an irrational inclination in him, one which his head forces him to declare as evidence of a physiologically transmitted insanity. The disease is in his blood, he believes, inherited from his immediate forebears, whereas Miss O'Connor would understand it not as a disease but as his heart's calling him beyond his fallen nature, thereby opening the possibility of a recovery. At every hand, creation threatens to plant mustard seed in Rayber's heart. But if his aberration from nature as he sees it is not a disease, neither is it a mistake of nature, as Rayber would have his idiot dependent, Bishop, to be in an attempt to preserve ideology. Rayber must inevitably find himself consumed by Old Tarwater's vision of creation if he cannot explain a literal idiot. The threat to Rayber is a visionary one in which the whole of creation, including even idiot children, becomes a sacramental mediator to God. Here is a passage from the novel to our point. In it, we see Rayber trying to exorcise his moments of love for the idiot child, Bishop, since those feelings of love make no sense to his threatened head. His sterile reason can understand such panic moments only as the onset of a madness foreshadowing his own complete madness. Hence the dilemma in the following passage:

> [His] normal way of looking on Bishop was as an x signifying the general hideousness of fate. He did not believe that he himself was formed in the image and likeness of God but that Bishop was he had no doubt. The little boy was part of a simple equation that required no further solution, except at the moments when with little or no warning he would feel himself overwhelmed by the horrifying love. Anything he looked at too long could bring it on. . . . It could be a stick or a stone, the line of a shadow, the absurd old man's walk of a starling crossing the sidewalk. If, without thinking, he lent himself to it, he would feel suddenly a morbid surge of love that terrified him—powerful enough to throw him to the ground in an act of idiot praise. It was completely irrational and abnormal. He was not afraid of love in general. . . . The love that would overcome him was of a different order entirely. It was not the kind that could be used for the child's improvement or his own. It was love without reason, love for something futureless, love that appeared to exist only to be itself, imperious and all demanding, the kind that would cause him to make a fool of himself in an instant.

Rather certainly, Miss O'Connor has reference in such passages as this to one of those moments of intersection of time by the timeless which are allowed us through grace, for that is the principal center of her art. And when she says that "The writer operates at a peculiar crossroads where time and place and eternity somehow meet," she means he does so, whether he realizes that "place" in its several dimensions or not. "His problem is to find that location," she adds, and in doing so a writer will come to see that the longer he looks at a particular thing, the more of the world and beyond the world he discovers in it. It is a lesson the maturing Eliot learned from Dame Julian of Norwich, and it allows Eliot to affirm with her in his last important poem that "all manner of thing shall be well." Dame Julian, in her *Revelations of Divine Love,* testifies to an encounter like those Tarwater and Rayber flee, with as slight an object in creation as a mule's rear or the absurd old man's walk of a starling. She reports a visionary moment God allowed her:

> he shewed [me] a little thing, the quantity of an hazel-nut, in the palm of my hand; and it was as round as a ball. I looked thereupon with eye of my understanding [i.e., her *intellectus,* heart] and thought: "What may this be?" And it was generally answered thus: "It is all that is made." I marvelled how it might last, for methought it might suddenly have fallen to naught for little[ness]. And I was answered in my understanding: "It lasteth, and ever shall [last] for that God loveth it." And so all thing hath the Being by the love of God.

We are, by our fallen natures, rather like Rayber; we are easily given to that love which can be used for self-improvement or the improvement of others, so long as we manage that improvement. Pragmatic love, whose use our world advances not only through sociologists such as Rayber but by sociologists like Marx and Lenin and Stalin as well, is an opiate we administer because it allows us to control agents in our manipulations of being. With such tolerance as the general opiate induces, we may be protected from the overwhelming threat of any violent love in pursuit of the kingdom of Heaven, the tragic intensity of willful being in such figures as the Misfit or young Tarwater. But in spite of our tolerant selves, there are those moments: the hazelnut held in our open palm, an old woman's gesture of unself-reflecting love, the line of a shadow, a spade or hoe; and we are lifted in a confusion whose message is "God loveth it," and that "all thing hath the Being by the love of God." Rayber, like most of us most of the time and some of us all of the time, can be comfortable with the givenness of creation only when allowed to define true love as an aberration of nature; concomitantly, he can be safe with trees only when he thinks of them as so many board feet. What makes trees as board feet acceptable to him is the abstraction by his thought which negates to the senses *woodness* itself. Particularity grounded in being is always dangerous, threatening us with a rescue of our life not dreamt of in our highway safety slogans. And so it becomes necessary to a Rayber to take refuge in reductionism managed by a rational intellect from which any influence of intuition, heart, has been exorcised by the will. The trees of Powderhead can be "loved" by Rayber as so many board feet converted to money for Tarwater's education. Otherwise, he must consent to the givenness in creation which cries out that "all thing hath the Being by the love of God." That way lies a surrender of the self which we speak of as love—when we speak truly of that state of our being. It is love that is the greatest terror of all, its violence the most destructive of the self.

I must not be misunderstood here. I do not mean at all that trees as board feet are not to be valued, that we may avoid that lesser violence in life that makes the practice of love in life—in the world—always excruciatingly complex for us. I mean rather to urge the necessity of a return to a sacramental sense in our acts of making, through which trees may be made into planks or rafters or firewood with due deference to their givenness. It is well to see that Rayber, in fact, is not a materialist, that indeed our age which we lament as materialistic has led us too easily to a pejorative coloring of our attitude toward material existence. We excoriate our materialistic age, but we are not so much materialists as abstractionists. We have modernized Manichaeanism in the interest of denying the givenness of creation. I am much struck by some observations of Philippe Aries in his *The Hour of Our Death.* In his chapter called "Avaritia and Still Life," he looks closely at the art of made things in the late Middle Ages and early Renaissance as those things reveal *avaritia*—that is, "the passionate and eager love of life, of persons as well as things." The danger in *avaritia* is the sinfulness which Dante characterizes as "excessive love" of things through the senses—but *excessive,* not *perverted.* From Aries's observations, however, we may discover that it has been a modern contribution to distort excessive love into perverted love, in Dante's sense of those two categories of sin. Aries observes that

> Before the thirteenth century the object is almost never regarded as a source of life, but rather as a sign, the symbolic representation of a movement [toward a transcendent existence]. . . . Beginning with

> the fourteenth century, objects are represented differently. It is not that they have ceased to be signs . . . but the relationship between the sign and its meaning has changed. . . . Things have invaded the abstract world of symbols. Each object has acquired new weight, proof of its autonomy.

When things regain an autonomy without losing their symbolic dimension in our eyes, we are healthfully balanced to withstand that gnostic temptation which reduces things to shadows of reality. Given that gnostic temptation, we do not value things as existing, as made through God's love. Aries is pointing to a moment's triumph in Western history of St. Thomas's good sense, reflected in our art before Ockham's nominalist confusions set in. When those confusions begin, our way of seeing things changes radically, and though Aries does not point to that nominalist intrusion as the beginning of that disorientation we call modernism, as Richard Weaver does, what Aries has to say about its effect on art and upon the meaning of materialism is revealing:

> contemplation and speculation, which characterize the psychology of the collector, are also the distinguishing traits of the protocapitalist, as he appears in the later Middle Ages and in the Renaissance. If we go back too far before capitalism, things do not yet deserve to be seen or held on to or desired. . . . wealth was not seen as the possession of things; it was identified with power over men just as poverty was identified with solitude. . . . If we go too far forward in capitalist evolution, the aptitude for speculation is preserved but the taste for contemplation disappears and there is no longer a sensual connection between man and his wealth. . . . Our industrial civilizations no longer believe that things possess a soul "which attaches itself to our soul and compels it to love." [The source of the medieval quotation is not given.] Things have become means of production, or objects to be consumed or devoured. They no longer constitute a "treasure." . . . Can one describe a civilization that has emptied things in this way as materialistic? On the contrary, it is the late Middle Ages, up to the beginning of modern times, that were materialistic! The decline in religious belief, in idealistic and normative morality, did not lead to the discovery of a more material world. Scientists and philosophers may lay claim to

> an understanding of matter, but the ordinary man in his daily life no more believes in matter than he believes in God, in life and in death, in the enjoyment of things and in their renunciation.

Let us make two observations on the passage, the first a modification that is not so signal to our concerns. Aries's use of the term *capitalism,* let me suggest, points to spectacle out of a pervasive fundamental spiritual change under way in the West. We need not trouble ourselves to accept or reject capitalism; what we should recognize is that a fundamental change is under way in the way we look at creation, a change involving ideas as various as those of Ockham, Descartes, Bacon, Locke. Rampant capitalism and rampant Marxism each have their origins in this distorted vision of man in nature and are a more symptomatic spectacle of our going astray than primary evidence of the dislocation.

The second observation is that the "Southernness" we are pursuing is very much given to the materialism Aries attributes to Western man at that point of balance when things were valued both speculatively and contemplatively, at a point approximately during the late Middle Ages. The love engendered through things involves our seeing into the heart of things, as Wordsworth was to put it in recognizing its loss; it involves our seeing "the dearest freshness deep down things," in Hopkins's phrase. If that rediscovery should lead an Ike McCaslin, in Faulkner's *Go Down, Moses,* to reject his calling to an active stewardship over those things that come to him from his fathers, he is rather exceptional. If more generally the Southerners we know are inclined to exploit things, especially now that we have a more progressive designation of ourselves as the Sun Belt (rather than the Bible Belt), it remains evident still that we hold, at least residually, that older view of the materiality of the world. We are attached to our homes, our garden, our pasture, our pickup trucks, and so on, and we are attached in a relationship that involves not only their speculative uses; they serve us contemplatively as well. We are still able to sense through such attachment that our souls are compelled to love things because things have their being by the love of God, as Dame Julian of Norwich saw. That is, our intuitive heart knows creation deeper than the head knows it, even if we cannot articulate that understanding or even when we are anxious to deny our understanding. That understanding has been historically a presence in our consciousness even when violated, as the land of the Deep South was violated in bleeding it for cotton, as humanity was violated through slavery. One finds this understanding, for instance, in William Byrd's writings; it is in John Taylor of Caroline County, and in John Randolph and many others. We need recalling ever to that known but forgotten attitude toward creation which Aries speaks of as the highest and most praiseworthy materialism. Nor can we ignore the fact that in such an attitude, as comforting as it sometimes is, lies always the threat of possession by love, a call to a surrender beyond the self which we see the Misfit and Rayber and Tarwater resisting. In that threat lies our best hope.

As artist, Miss O'Connor very much appreciates the temptation to which we are given, our reluctance to surrender to the cause of existence through existence itself, for fear we lose the little painful world of the isolated self. That hesitation leaves one dramatically poised, as is her Misfit in "A Good Man Is Hard to Find," between doing meanness and giving up all in that surrender which is love. He is poised between destroying every *res* encountered, either by force of intellect or physical violence, and treasuring everything from the lilies of the valley and fallen sparrows even unto our lowly, down-home homely possum. What the Misfit and Rayber alike struggle against is the admission that, in every moment of their being, they operate as creative (albeit flawed) agents, rather than as causes of *esse* or causes of being. To their frustration, neither can they unmake being, except partially their own. Since one who can only participate in his existence through being cannot be the first cause of existence itself, he may rage against his secondary role in existence, but he cannot change the reality that he is already created before he can even imagine himself a creator. Any address to the mundane is doomed by presumptuousness from the first morning in the Garden, where we first failed to catch this possum. We fail when we do not first acknowledge existence to be a gift not caused by the possum hunt. A modification of that eager presumptuousness was made by the Puritan fathers, the presumption that man is the agent of grace in nature. That distortion was raised toward a virtue by some of the New England divines, the generators not only of Pragmatism—Puritanism secularized—but of our homegrown existentialists as well. Of course, given our willfulness, it is difficult to accept a role as merely participator in the ground of being rather than its cause. That is the shattering point Miss O'Connor's Hulga wrecks upon, to her good fortune no doubt, in "Good Country People." The shattering rock is the Bible salesman, one of those homegrown Existentialists who has not needed a doctorate in philosophy to be able to believe in nothingness.

My view of the matter, and I believe Miss O'Connor's and St. Thomas's and Mr. Eliot's and Donald Davidson's—each with refinements in his view out of each's peculiar personhood—may be stated as a conclusion to this first of our possum hunts. Though man be given a freedom, through which he may easily delude himself into believing himself the first or the sole or primary cause of his free actions of creation (as Rayber for instance insists upon), reason itself will tell him if he but listen that he is himself a given. Even his freedom is a given. In this view, there can be no such thing as the self-made man, as Emerson preached: only the self-unmade man, the first in our long history of unmakings usually spoken of under the name Old Adam. For whatever the nature of man's actions as "maker," whatever his calling, he is always operating *upon* givens, *with* givens, and *out of* his own givenness. That is always a great shock of a conclusion to come to, given the self-elevation our pride attempts. Nor is it a conclusion provided only to the heroes of art and history. In the continuum of our becoming, the recognition strikes us again and again, with an effect almost as disturbing as those elevated Keatsean or Augustinian moments. What it shares with those high moments, I suspect, when we come closer to understanding the experience with heart and mind in concert, is that ours has been, for a moment at least, a recovery of known but forgotten things. It is the shock of the expected in those self-righting, visionary moments.

Two

POSSUMS IN THE IN-BETWEEN

As a Thomist would put it, *possum* principles exist in a manner separate from my conception of those principles; they exist independent of my conception. The *res significandi* (the thing signified) and the *modus significandi* (the way in which it is signified) differ, and if I persist in confusing the two concepts, *possumness* will remain unaffected, though I myself shall be thrown into confusion. As a particular scholastic commentator puts it, in examining the relation between existence and causality, "a real community of nature in things precedes the logical community of concepts in our minds."[1] And because of that community of nature that binds creation, we must commit ourselves to pursue an understanding of that binding. Our modern refusal is the rejection of any commitment to metaphysics, a refusal made easy by the assumption that concepts in our mind precede any real community in nature. We make, each his own, an *ad hoc* metaphysics sufficient unto the moment. Order thus becomes the mind's prerogative, the imposition of which upon that anomalous chaos which is separate from our particular mind is declared the ultimate creation. Put as Jean-Paul Sartre would put it, being is the effect of action. But this means there are as many worlds as there are consciousnesses.

If the Sartrean should come to that conclusion, he finds himself hoisted on his own eager presumption: for it is evident that he must conclude that there can be only the one world of his own making and not multiple worlds; he must also say that all other consciousnesses exist solely because of his making. It is little wonder that, through such clever and sometimes witty nonsense, the several world—that is, the multiplicity of existences, particularly of individual man—is in chaos and mind itself haunted by its alienation unto itself. That alienation alone allows the modernist mind like Sartre's some pretense to the heroic agony of mind, angst having been made the highest good. There is a philosophical sentimentality involved in this gradual translation of Milton's Satan into the Prometheus of Aeschylus. We deal, though, with a translation, not a transmutation of the thing itself. The logical manipulation of concepts in the mind does not issue in an actual restructuring of the community of being in nature. What does result, however, is heroic self-righteousness in which a willful alienation from existence is declared virtue rather than sin.

If my pursuit of *possumness* abused seems far-fetched, removed from our pursuit of "Southernness" into a byway of French intellectual history, we need only recall some of Miss O'Connor's characters: Hulga, Ashbury, Julian, Haze Motes, for instance. She shows us repeatedly Southern characters gone astray after such newfangledness. As for her own position, she believes along with our commentator on the *Summa* of St. Thomas that to say that things exist commits us to a metaphysical pursuit of endless analogy in existence. The longer we look at a single thing, the more of the world we see in it. The more of the world we see in the hazelnut or mule's rear or starling's old-man walk, the more we cry out for the cause of analogy, the cause of kinship in creation. The existence of that hunger "can never be satisfied merely to begin but requires to pour out its substance in search of achievement and fulfillment."[2] One is committed to ends beyond Five-Year Plans or Thousand-Year Ends by the very acceptance of existence as preceding action, by the very act of reaching toward the created world; the gesture in itself acknowledges creation's existence as separate from, though inclusive of, our reaching. And this acknowledgment is implicit even when the gestures are acts of violence against existence.

What I must emphasize here, given the philosophical cast of my argument at this point, is that we are not called, each of us, to be philosopher. We are nevertheless each given impetus to metaphysical understanding, to the seeing of community in being and a reaching toward fulfillment of a delegated existence. It is an inevitable consequence of that special gift of being we call our humanity. It is Miss O'Connor's genius, or rather one should say her special gift, to have recognized this impetus in us. She dramatizes it, perhaps more effectively through her natural philosophers than in her pseudo- or semieducated philosophers. The child in "The River," Nelson in "The Artificial Nigger," Haze Motes or the two Tarwaters—all these dramatize my point that intellectual sophistication is not necessarily the means toward metaphysical understanding; Hulga, Julian, Rayber, Ashbury on the other hand rather suggest that pseudointellectualism, the worship of the *ratio* to the exclusion of the *intellectus,* is most dangerous indeed to a profound encounter with being and the Cause of being. Those characters she speaks of as "natural Catholics," like Old Tarwater, have advantages in their struggle to recover reality that the deracinated intellectuals do not. For it is a reason denatured that the pseudointellectual embraces. Reason denatured, divorced from the gift of our complex being, succumbs to that oldest temptation of all, the desire as Genesis puts it to "be as the gods."

Perhaps our excursion into the philosophy of being here will help explain why I am fearful of transgression when I take those concepts as they are in my mind as cause of being in things themselves. My ideas when they are fresh in mind do seem to take precedence over principles of reality; that error I fear more than any violation of patents or copyrights. I am fearful because, in clearer moments, I am aware of effects upon our civilization resulting from our having known but forgotten these simple home truths. The woodsman knows that trees precede his ax, which wisdom in extension saves him from severed toes and falling trees. For our world's ideologists, however, the idea is a thing to be used independent of home truths, independent of our native understanding of the relation of existence and causality. Ideals thus become idols, through the worship of which we become gnostic manipulators of being. Through idols held in common comes that terrible focus of power over nature and man. For some ideologists, particularly the more effective among them, know most surely those flaws in our given nature that make us susceptible to worshipping idols, that inclination which perverts our desire to pour out the substance of our existence in pursuit of fulfillment. The gnostic's focus of power through idol worship is an attempt to foreshorten the unfolding of our being, to rush history—individual and community. This is the inclination in us, at a seemingly harmless level, which Miss O'Connor speaks of in relation to the reader who demands that his heart be lifted up by her fiction:

> There is something in us, as storytellers and as listeners to stories, that demands the redemptive act, that demands that what falls at least be offered the chance to be restored. The reader of today looks for this motion, and rightly so, but what he has forgotten is the cost of it. His sense of evil is diluted or lacking altogether, and so he has forgotten the price of restoration. When he reads a novel, he wants either his senses tormented or his spirits raised. He wants to be transported, instantly, either to a mock damnation or a mock innocence.[3]

Now the gnostic manipulator of being, the one who would use ideas as a magician's wand over man and nature, though he disbelieve in the God of Abraham nevertheless believes in this innate hunger of substance for fulfillment; he accepts a teleological drive in human nature and sees it evidenced particularly in the "ideological" inclination of man toward millennial ends. He will nevertheless explain it in terms of mechanistic evolution. At his best, that is, he is only perverse philosopher, perhaps withdrawn into the acid of cynicism. At his worst, he recognizes the terrible power of ideology when it is under collective control by a subtle mind. On the one hand, he must deny that our inclination to worship idols is a truncation of a higher calling in us lest his authority prove derivative. On the other hand, he must encourage idol worship in order to enlist the power of that hunger in us. If he does not "sincerely" encourage such worship, he is in danger of being found out. Then he should have to declare honestly that the inclination is a fiction he encourages as a means to his own ends. In turn—if honest—he must account for the inclination in mechanistic terms. He must at least admit or deny that it is he who dreams a perfection which he intends to impose. Since in our several mind there is not one but many gnostic dreams, he must confront the ultimate question: Why your dream rather than mine? We must ask, if we accept the actual premise of his operation of mind; namely, his denial of logic or purpose in existence itself when existence is divorced from the human mind.

Of course, if we look closely we shall discover this gnostic manipulator of being tipping his hand at this point. If an Emerson can say, "The world is nothing, the man is all," he will presently say, "the firmament flows before [such a man], and takes his signet and form." It is but one step then to the declaration that "He is great who can alter my state of mind." Such a great mind must give itself to "the stern ambition to be the Self of the nation and of nature." He must "cast behind [him] all conformity, and acquaint men at first hand with Deity. Be to them a man." In short, that man is not only an ideologue, but the idol as well, the "Deity" of the nation and nature who declares that "Nothing is at last sacred but the integrity of our own mind." And the words *he* and *our* mean nothing in such a climate of thought till translated to *I*. We cannot turn aside from the recognition that in Emerson's words lie a prophecy of the New Man raised to shocking presence in our world. I shall play Enoch Emory to Emerson's Haze Motes by pointing out that Emerson's version of the Church Without Christ has its New Jesuses in profusion: Emerson's description of the calling and authority of the New Man fits with shocking appropriateness Joseph Stalin and Adolph Hitler, among others.[4]

The secular gnostic, the one "born Yankee of the race of men," the deadly enemy of that "Southernness" I would rescue, has learned from Nietzsche, as Marx and Lenin quickly learned, that mankind is addicted to dreams of heaven—even as he must labor to explain that addiction as an effect of misguided history rather than of an intuitive right-mindedness. He must then confuse our will in this matter if our will is to be redirected by us to gnostic ends. Thus religion as an opiate of the people is a most welcome drug to the gnostic New Man intent himself on being the new divinity, "the Self of the nation and of nature." The perversion of that intuitive hunger for divinity—our hunger to be reunited, lifted up—is the most certain way to ideological ends, needing only the consent of our impatience. The gnostic ideologue thus directs our attention toward a dreamed-of perfection in time, which he colors to attract the idealistic inclinations in us as one colors sugar water with Red Dye Number 2 to attract hummingbirds. It is thus that he may command and accumulate the continuing spiritual energy in us, our individual power which when healthily employed through right-mindedness leads us toward final truths rather than into fanciful dreams.

Now words are the crucial instrument to the gnostic New Man. The energy of collective mind as it may be harnessed through words is at issue, and those minds span our gifts individually taken, from the intellectual to the submental. It must include even those remote minds resident in the outland South, those of possum infamy, the alternative being to exclude such minds, setting them aside as a few are set aside on Reservations in Huxley's *Brave New World.* But such reservations will always be a danger. That outland, that "Southern," mind has proved most resistent to ideological controls that posit temporal ends as ultimate ends, a point effectively argued by Richard Weaver in several of his writings. The necessity of establishing powerful control over common sense if gnostic restructurings of mind are to be effective has been repeatedly illustrated in our century by totalitarian actions against common sense. There is Stalin's deliberate starvation of the Kulaks—Russia's "Southern" yeomanry—in the 1930s, the horrors of which are only now being reluctantly recognized and acknowledged in the West. More recently, though still distant to most of us, has been the systematic slaughter of Cambodians by the Khmer Rouge. There are at the present moment similar undertakings in Afghanistan and in Ethiopia, though it is easier to be sentimental about starving children in Ethiopia than to engage through significant action the causes of starvation. It will cost us dearly to admit that ideological manipulations of nature in the East and on the African continent are inescapable causes of wholesale destruction of the creatures there.[5]

WORDS are the ready instruments of ideological manipulation. *Words* relate to *ideas* as ideas relate to *reality,* and the complex relation of these three elements is most clearly revealed to us in our community through the signs of community, through language held in common. To hold language in common does not imply nor require that language be taken only at its most elementary level, of course, at the level of traffic directions. In community, we range through slang and colloquialism to a variety of the formal—from poetry's symbols to science's. And there is a constant infusion at each level from all others, meaning that it is in the use of language that we must be most careful insofar as we attempt to establish individual and community integrity and purpose.

Now language is the poet's especial concern; for him it becomes almost the end in itself, his attention primarily on finding the right word. As maker, his concern is for the good of the thing he makes, and that thing is an existence—a "being"—of words. But it does not follow that the poet is not concerned with words as mediator between idea and reality. If he is not so concerned, his words will be but empty, his poems opaque symbols, as some modern poetry has tended to be. I have in mind as instance the sort of deadend that words come to in the French Symbolist Movement. Mallarmé's and Dante's uses of "symbols" are radically different, as poets like Pound and Eliot and Tate quickly realized. This recognition helps account for the enlarging address to the world through words which the Vanderbilt Fugitives moved toward as they became "Agrarians." We remember that John Crowe Ransom wrote not only *Chills and Fever* but also *God without Thunder;* in the prose work he opposes empty language, words that, being thunder without God, fade to tinkling ornaments, become as sounding brass.

Those young Fugitives began to realize the South besieged by advocates of various Five-Year Plans aimed at emptying nature and man, and they realized that not all such plans were advanced by the multiplying varieties of Socialists becoming dominant in the Western World after World War I. Short-range increments are more appealing than millennial measures to the emotions in individuals. Heaven on earth is a more attractive concept than that of eternity in our pursuit of ultimate fulfillment, given especially our impatience with time itself. In totalitarian societies, economic and social programs advanced with the authority of science and structured incrementally can be made to seem reasonable at first, but not at last, to the meanest of minds. In politically free societies, even periodic elections may serve a similar function, as our recent encounters with New Frontiers and Great Societies might remind us. When one adds to this appeal to our impatient pursuit of Heaven the principle of consumerism as the highest good, confusion of ends is confounded, a point we should keep in mind whenever we see statistics comparing the cost of a Soviet automobile and the Soviet citizen's prospects of access to an automobile with our own superiority in respect to these goods. Again, I do not reject automobiles, only the subtle confusion of goods as the ultimate end of life. In this context, we should not be surprised that the Agrarians were and are attacked from all quarters, left and right.

If I am even partially correct in this assessment of our predilection to ideology, it warns me that the ideas I advance must be properly seen in relation to principles of reality which are independent of my ideas of them. That is, whatever *idea* I take to mind through principles perceived in reality, the principles themselves are not affected by that taking. I may or may not, through my ideas, be truly oriented to reality, though it is inevitable that if my ideas are wrongly taken from reality or wrongly used against reality, reality itself will at some point reassert itself. For reality is no respector of wayward mind. To say the idea in a cliché: the tree falls separate from whether I hear it or not, or whether having heard it I deny the experience. Less metaphorically, the principles of vegetation operate in spite of Lysenko's and Stalin's declarations, as the history of Soviet agriculture demonstrates.

I mean to assert here that the truth resident in the reality of being is ultimately the measure of thought and not our thought the measure of truth. Although we are forever inclined to the contrary through willfulness, we are not the dictators of reality. We might suppose (the fifth-grade teacher used to tell us) that the cat's tail is a fifth leg. We may *will* to think it a leg, even if the cat can't walk on it. We may assert that a frog with all its legs cut off can't hear when we shout at it to jump. Of course, as we become more deeply engaged by the matrix of reality, engaged in the drama of ourselves thrown into existence, we should discover ourselves less certain about the number of feet a creature has. Take our possum's tail in contrast to the cat's. Prehensile, we know. It holds onto the world, from the possum's point of view perhaps. And to the young kit just freed of the pouch, we may imagine that the mama's tail seems a steadying hand in an unsteady world; it may even seem the axis of the universe. We may even imagine an analogy: here is the worried little face of the white beast kit, its tail curled about its mother's tail, swinging upside down with its paws clinging to that coarse brittle fur. Now consider the distressed face of a three-year-old child clinging to its mother's well-manicured hand in a busy Macon or Atlanta mall. The analogy is not so outrageous but that a poet might make something of it. From such imaging it is not difficult to move on to a conclusion that the act of imaging, and the ideas out of the mind's metaphorical friction between images, are instruments that determine reality: our words extended from mind make reality. We have the authority of Emerson, as we have said, for such a progress toward confusion. All that is NOT ME, says Emerson, all that is not my consciousness is an "apparition," a shadow of my consciousness. The "apparition," he insists, includes his own body. "The world is nothing, the man is all." Thus is gnostic man "made Providence [i.e., God] to himself, dispensing good to his goodness, and evil to his sins." "He who knows that power is in the soul . . . works miracles." He does so by becoming the New Man with "the stern ambition to be the Self of the nation and of nature."

But against such false platitude, reality reasserts itself, shocking us back to our common sense. In juxtaposing the three-year-old to the possum kit, each clinging to its mother, I begin to border on that province of mind whose right order is threatened by sentimentality. If by equation we show correspondences reasonable, if the six-week-old kit is the "equivalent" in its development to the three- or four-year-old child, if we are moved to anguish by the child's worried face and detect therefrom anguish in the possum kit's face, if we are against child abuse, it will not be long before a committee of the anguished form a "Preserve Our Possum" movement. They will put up possum-crossing signs on the highways, even picket our entrepreneur's frisbees and Pogo Burgers. Sentiment gets out of hand pretty quickly. That is to say, a proper sentiment directed toward creation becomes perverse. Popular versions of science (the analogies in infanthood between child and possum) as modified by an imagination escaping reality into the clouds of fancy often lead us to curious predicaments. Valid thought in such a climate of mind bogs down. The danger is real that I may distort my understanding of reality by my biased view of it and so become disoriented. Meanwhile, reality continues unaffected. Mama possums keep having baby possums and not little girls.

I wish to engage this danger of a distorted understanding of reality, in part because it is the warning accusation brought against the Agrarians, and particularly against Donald Davidson. His accusers range from the ignorant, through the facile, to the perverse, though the common theme in the accusation is the same, inevitably ending in a cliché: Davidson and the Agrarians do not see the real world, they wish "to turn the clock back." This quoted cliché is precisely the one directed at Davidson by Ralph McGill in his *Atlanta Constitution* column; the accusation used to appear once a year, as predictably as McGill's annual spring bucolic paean to Virgil's *Georgics* and that poem's description of bee keeping and the wisdom of crop rotation. Whether Allen Tate and Donald Davidson better understand Virgil than Ralph McGill is a lecture in itself which I must forgo, being intent at the moment upon baby possums, small children, and the dangers of sentiment's turning into sentimentality. I must then turn with my point to Donald Davidson's own citation in his first Lamar Lecture of the editorial response of the *Macon Telegraph* (September 23, 1930) to the publication of *I'll Take My Stand.* At the time of the editorial, the book itself had not yet appeared. The editorial asserts that these "Neo-Confederates" are "a socially reactionary band [who want] horses and buggies and music boxes to replace automobiles and radios." By labeling the Agrarian position as one of nostalgic sentimentality, the editorial advances its own sentimentality through the words it chooses. Those words suggest that the editorialist equates the good life with automobiles and radios. But time passes, bringing the coloring of nostalgia upon the editorial itself in consequence, though the writer did not recognize its incipient presence as he wrote the words. For, caught in the moment's fad, one is likely to think rather approvingly of that faddishness as evidence of an advanced, progressive address to the world. The editorialist celebrating the automobile and radio in the 1930s may be seen in the 1980s as content to arrest the clock of progress, since the latest, if lateness be its virtue, becomes merely the old with inexorable time. Clearly, we now have the better life, with stratojets and cable TV.

The rhetorical principle of the editorial intends to frighten the growing consumer mind with the loss of consumer conveniences if it pay heed to that strange Nashville crowd. John Q, as the editorial cartoonist would have him called, may lose the fruits of science if he gives ear to radical antediluvians like Donald Davidson and his lot. Next those weird oldies will be arguing that we should give up patio gas braziers and even perhaps air conditioning. Certainly we have progressed since the most ancient of radicals, Socrates, insisted that the unexamined life is not worth living. But what haunts us in our day is the recognition that increasingly we can tolerate life only when it is made safe from examination, when it is reduced to goods and conveniences.

What Davidson and the Agrarians were being accused of by the editorial writer of the *Telegraph*, and subsequently by Ralph McGill in the *Constitution,* was a sentimentality which ignored "reality." But their argument itself depends upon a sentimentality which removes the accusers, not putatively but actually, from reality. Of course terms like *reality* and *sentimentality* come trippingly to the tongue in any public engagement of minds over social or spiritual questions; that is, whenever that power resident in the public mind is being wooed. It becomes important, then, to be quite clear what one means by such terms. I wish to define *sentimentality* as opposed to that most valuable deportment in us, *sentiment.* Both are climates of the mind derived from and accountable to reality. As for the term *reality,* its meaning will emerge cumulatively from the beginning of these lectures to the point where I shall presently characterize it with the help of Eric Voegelin.

Sentiment, let us say, is that spiritual climate of one's being when one is ordinately in love with creation. That is to say, sentiment is that deportment of our spirit toward creation which results when we have found our proper relation to both being—creation—and the cause of being—the Creator. Its source to us as a word is from Latin, through medieval Latin to French, and thence into English after the Battle of Hastings. The Latin verb means "to feel," and I believe it safe to suggest it appropriate to relate it to that other medieval Latin word already introduced, the *intellectus* as distinct from the *ratio*—that knowledge of the heart which differs from the knowledge of the head. For it is of coordinate interest to observe that our word *sentinel* comes from the same Latin verb which gives us *sentiment,* though mediated through Italian to French. It is not amiss to suggest that sentiment is that guard in the spirit—sustained by the *intellectus,* the heart—that keeps the *ratio* orderly when it would otherwise turn tyrant. If a "realist" should object to my analogy of possum kit to little girl, on the grounds that such metaphor can be merely sentimental, his would be an understandable objection, given the perversions of sentiment that abound. The organization of a Society for the Prevention of Cruelty to Possums would be strong evidence to his point. After all, he might protest, little possums at first sight seem creatures even a mother possum must find hard to love. But such an objection, protesting that excessive response to analogy which distorts sentiment into sentimentality, misunderstands that analogy may be properly anchored in reality and therefore supportive of sentiment, even as it may be improperly anchored so that it distorts our vision of reality.

At a more volatile level, this realist's misunderstanding makes it difficult to argue with him on such questions as abortion or pornography, ideas about which there is considerable rage in the public spirit, not excluding sentimentality on both sides of the issues. As for the aesthetic dimension, the argument *ad possum* that declares the small ugly creature beyond a mother's love, perhaps we may lay it to rest at once with St. Thomas's definition of beauty. Beauty is "that which, when seen, pleases." But as always, the meanings of the terms are decisive, to Thomas's eyes depending not at all upon an unexamined impressionism. Thomas would insist that, if the possum is seen for what it is, as opposed to what might at the moment please our disordered sensibilities in response to it, even it must be conceded beautiful. That is, insofar as it is a creature true in its actuality to its potential, true to its *possumness,* it would be both irrational, not to say un-Christian, to conclude it ugly in and of itself. The appropriateness of its being will please the rational intellect, and rational intellect would find itself supported by sentiment. If the creature in itself seems grotesque—if upon our initial encounter with it, it seems rather a creation by a government committee than by the mystery of the Creator's actions—we misunderstand the grotesque. We won't be able to recognize a freak when we see one. The possum is not an aberration of being, and our initial repulsion, if that is our response, is caused by our senses being disorganized in relation to our sentiment. To hold the possum repugnant is but the obverse of being so moved by its difficulties on the highways as to form militant preservation societies. Of course, we usually have quicker and longer memories for militantly and mushy sentimentality than for that species of sentimentality that parades under the guise of an indifferent realism. We remember longer, for instance, Eleanor Roosevelt on migratory waterfowl than we will remember our possum scoffer. On learning certain horrors that migratory birds suffer on their long journey south in winter and north in spring, she asked, "Couldn't *something* be done? Perhaps change their habits?"[6]

If we define sentiment as the spiritual climate of one's being when one is ordinately in love with creation, how shall we define sentimentality? I suggest that it is that vaporous climate of mind out of confused thought and feeling which drifts into an inordinate love of creation—of being. Or, alternately, it is a peremptory rejection of being, save one's own. For we must not overlook the cynics as sentimentalists; I would provide a circle in Hell, were I Dante, where the two manifestations must perpetually engage each other: a Mrs. Roosevelt and an Ambrose Bierce at a perpetual tea. Sentimentality, then, is a mode of *deportment* toward creation, revealed through word and gesture, and not necessarily a mode of *action* toward it.[7] The sentimentalist's attitude toward general creation in general gives a greater importance to the circumstances of his own being—his individual existence—than is warranted by the complexity of creation. Put in St. Thomas's or Dante's terms, sentimentality is an effect in the soul of pride. It trades on analogy, on seeing likeness in unlike things. Now all our attempts to come to terms with multitudinous creation must engage analogy, but sentimentality trades on such correspondences at the surface of likeness and consequently at the expense of being taken only as its individual manifestations. That is why one Mother Teresa gives the lie to a multitude of the boisterously charitable in a collective giving.

Perhaps I may make my distinction between sentiment and sentimentality clearer by introducing two species of sentimentality whose excesses are rather obvious. The first we recognize at once, and it is the one we are most likely to admit succumbing to ourselves. It is also the one most easy to make fun of. That we are generally victims of this sentimentality is evident from the wealth of well-wisher cards at any local stationer. One might design for these, this membership of Sentimentalists International, a card based on things we've already said. A mama possum, tail arched over her back, to which clings a baby possum clinging upside down, its fingered paws grasping her fur. (If one of you markets this card, beware of my copyright.) Of course the little creature should be grinning with a cute little face, since any hint of terror in its expression dooms sales. On the other hand, depending on our artist's inclination to acknowledge the existence of our possum realist, the mama possum might be wearing a long-suffering look rather than a mama's smile. The possum realist anticipated by such a fillip may well be the parent of the child to whom the card is sent. She will have picked up the card from the mailbox after an exhausting tour of the mall, towing her even more exhausted three-year-old. Inside the card are the words, "So! Today you're three!" Exclamation point! There is white space for Maiden Aunt Sophia to write a personal note to the child, and perhaps even an aside to her mother. At the least she must sign her name. The printed part is to be read to the nonpossum child by the mother, who will smile or not, depending upon the morning.

For convenience, we'll call this form of sentimentality the Hallmark Greeting Card Variety. If evidence of sentiment gone wrong in figures cutely drawn and verses destructive of all poetry, it nevertheless proceeds from a legitimate sentiment. We can deal with such wayward sentiment knowingly, the displays of which we have been teasing. We can even go ahead and send the possum card ourselves. But what are we to do for a drawing and a message ready-made when we discover a close friend consumed by cancer? That is the point where, sentimentality having become habitual in us, we meet reality head-on and are devastated and confused. Dislocated sentiment is suddenly exposed to the sharp and jagged edges of reality and deflated, leaving heart and mind empty and helpless. For if it is especially difficult for us to deal with that evil in creation manifested in our world by psychopathic, serial murderers, what are we to do when confronted by wild cells? Carcinogens have become almost a welcome relief, since they allow us for a moment to put aside ultimate engagements with evil, expecting each day science's rescue.

We need reminding, no doubt, that it is not random coincidence nor simply accident that ready-made greeting cards are an invention of the Victorian Age; the first ones apparently were sent on Valentine's Day. They are not bequeathed us by those notorious "Other Victorians" recently discovered to have inhabited the dark underside of the Victorian era, those who distorted beauty into gruesome aberrations. While in the front parlor one was embarrassed to speak of the leg or thigh of a chicken, upstairs or down in a darkened room flesh and bone alike were being savaged in perverse delight. I have a theory, worth a grant from the National Endowment for the Humanities perhaps, that the popular romance novel of our day manages to combine both sorts of distortion of the beauty of existence, combines both aspects of sentimentality. That romance novels are vastly popular in our day ought, if my theory prove right, to be cause for alarm.

Having mentioned the Other Victorians brings me, then, to a second species of sentimentalist whom I propose to label the *Playboy* Magazine Variety. Again, the distortion of sentiment practiced by this species is prompted by an inordinate love, as is the Hallmark Species. That is, neither engages being at the level of reality. As for the *Playboy* Variety, out of an excessive hunger for the things of the world, he colors the surface of things luridly, his paint softened by the excited juices of appetite. Here is that distortion of reality whose art we commonly call pornography. But this distortion, too, is out of pride when one sees it from the orthodox address of sentiment to reality which I maintain is healthfully "Southern." God made the world at and in His pleasure; this *Playboy* sentimentalist of bodily functions chooses to deconstruct the high meaning in the term *pleasure* through a carcinoid appetite. He would devour reality; most immediately and often with perverse naiveté he devours the reality of his own being.

Please notice: I am not speaking here merely of that private, secret sentimentality of appetite which used occasionally to shock us when discovered by accident within the community. Such randomly lost souls are always with us. I'm concerned that such a random soul should declare itself a movement, advance its mode of sentimentality as a public alternative, as a "life-style" to be accepted as legitimate to the realities of nature. Hugh Hefner sometime back began a campaign through a series of maunderings in *Playboy* that purported to be a new philosophical justification for sensuality, attempting thereby to recruit sentiment to his cause under the pretense of reason. His is an instance of the *ratio* turned randomly upon the world through a corruption of language. I do not mean here his advocacy of vigorous Anglo-Saxon words that are a schoolboy's rightful inheritance. I mean rather his pretense to a precision of thought in relation to reality, expressed with the full force of the mind's logic in relation to nature's logic. Hugh Hefner as philosopher is at best caricature of philosopher, though he was taken seriously by the vulnerable.

Ordinarily, one finds these two species of sentimentalists blindly antagonistic to each other, the *Playboy* Variety and the Hallmark Variety. The publishers of *Hustler, Penthouse,* and *Playboy* from the beginning depend upon shocking news stories to sell themselves. The putative target of their brand of high seriousness about the legitimacy of excessive appetite was largely the proper (in the Victorian sense) sentimentalist. But the seemingly primary object, one suspects, was only proximate to the real target—those already disoriented by but increasingly antagonistic to what we may call a front parlor sentimentality. The intended audience was not old but young possums. That the time for such a movement was right is suggested by general community turmoil over the question of pornography in the hands and glands of the young. That these liberated sentimentalist editors of *Playboy* read the community situation correctly is attested to by their circulation figures.[8] I have already suggested, however, that the two sentimentalities are compatible, as in the paperback romance novel reader. And I dare say there are *Penthouse* or *Playboy* readers who send possum birthday cards. On occasion, events conspire to bring them together in public attention, at which time we see the kinship between them in their abuse of reality.

BOTH the *Hallmark* and the *Playboy* species of sentimentality, we have prepared to say, depend upon unbridled imagination, which once liberated from reason and dominating our intuition, turns sentiment inside out. For sentiment, as we have defined it, is another term for love, for *agape.* It orients us to an open but proportionate response to both creation and to the cause of creation. The imagination, when governed by heart and head in consort, makes the soul thrive through analogy, so that there is a feasting of form in the mind, that informing of mind being the process whereby we come into our potential. It is not Wordsworth who first celebrates the action of our senses in nature through which the spark of the imagination reveals to us that we participate in the being of the thing perceived. Wordsworth puts it that participation is action within the mighty world of the senses, in which world we half perceive and half create the object sensed. If that outburst of reflective vision in "Tintern Abbey" rests in words somewhat shakily used, insofar as the philosopher might credit them, Wordsworth is rather surely on the verge of understanding the role of our senses in nature and of the part played by such action in moving us toward the larger Cause that binds perceiver and perceived. He is not, I dare venture, so far from St. Thomas in what he is attempting to argue as his imprecise language might suggest.

Perhaps I may introduce here Herbert McCabe's commentary on St. Thomas's idea of knowledge toward rescuing Wordsworth—at least the Wordsworth of "Tintern Abbey"—from suspicions of either Platonic Idealism or pagan Deism. For Thomas, what is intelligible about things is their form, form being that in virtue of which a thing actually is what it is. Form allows the thing to be intelligible, and in respect to the multiplicity of forms in things, the mind provides a place where form may be and yet be unencumbered by matter. In this respect, form has a real presence in mind, though Wordsworth's description of form "in-pressed," of the mind as "in-formed," may seem too literal in his understanding. That is, we recognize in him an immediate resort, in respect to teleology, to recent thinkers like John Locke and David Hartley. St. Thomas holds, in McCabe's words, that in the act of perceiving "both the senses and the sensible thing are realized together." In Thomas's own words, "The sense in act *is* the sensible in act." The words have a very Wordsworthean ring to them, though they do not carry the passion of imaginative discovery that is in Wordsworth's lines.

What St. Thomas is exploring here we might see dramatized in the life of one of our favorite saints, one popular with the secular as well as the religious mind. I mean St. Francis of Assisi. What St. Thomas is intent on establishing, however, is that it is through this play between mind and thing that mind itself realizes its potential. He is putting the rational argument that supports that active participation in being which we celebrate in St. Francis; Wordsworth celebrates it in himself. As McCabe puts it, "form in the mind actualizes the mind itself," the only mind not requiring that actualization being God's. Man's mind, which is the lowest kind of intelligence (to which we contrast the angelic mind), "before it can actually exist needs to be informed. . . . the mind realizes its own capacity by realizing the capacity of . . . nature to be intelligible." Again, in Thomas's own words, "The understanding in act *is* the intelligible in act." And we must recognize here the importance of "understanding." To know is primary to the *ratio;* to understand to the *intellectus*—the head and heart, respectively.

With this thrust of Thomas's argument, we may at once appreciate the importance of his other contention that we are moved toward God first of all through the response of our senses. Taking into the mind the logical forms of nature, through analogy, we are moved toward an encounter with perfect form, that form which is both the cause of and independent of informed nature. But we appreciate also the capacity of mind in the manipulation of form, through which manipulation form is divorced from the *res significata* (the thing signified) and the *modus significandi* (the way in which it is signified) in the mind. Form so divorced becomes, not actual form in the mind, but form reduced to abstraction by the will. The erstwhile actions of imagination, through which mind participates in the reality of existences, becomes fancy. While Coleridge is exacting in his distinctions, he is perhaps not entirely orthodox in them. The fancy, he says, "is indeed no other than a mode of Memory emancipated from the order of time and space." It plays with "fixities and definites," though like ordinary memory its materials are "made from the law of association." The secondary imagination, on the other hand, in its poetic operation "dissolves, diffuses, dissipates, in order to recreate. . . . it struggles to idealize and to unify." When St. Thomas says that the artist imitates not nature but the operation of nature, one may see a correspondence between his point and Coleridge's description of the creative activity of the secondary imagination in dealing with the mind's materials "made from the law of association." Orthodox or no, what is rather certain is that Coleridge does not allow the imagination to divorce the ideal form it strives for from actual existence, even though he does declare that, while the imagination is "essentially vital"—life-giving through form—"all objects (*as* objects) are essentially fixed and dead." It is in this reduction of being in things—objects—that Coleridge deviates more widely from Thomas than does Wordsworth.

Coleridge sees a threatening perversity in fancy which may disengage the forms in memory from their origins in objects. That would be to separate mind from reality. Fancy may do so, as Coleridge recognizes, "by that empirical phenomenon of the will, which we express by the word CHOICE." The secondary imagination, however, deals in analogues to *res significata,* the forms in the mind, and is dependent from the primary imagination, which in turn is "the living Power and prime Agent of all human Perception, and as a repetition in the finite mind of the eternal act of creation in the infinite I AM." It is in this anchor of the primary imagination in the Cause of all existence that Coleridge acknowledges man's being created in the image of God; his emphasis upon man as maker—as poet—follows from the acknowledgment. And if it were clear that he means by those ideas and fixed "objects" the form suspended in memory rather than things independent of mind, we would have a yet closer approximation of Coleridge's description of the creative activity of the imagination to Thomas's statement that art is an imitation of the action of nature and not an imitation of nature itself. We see that in Coleridge's argument the secondary imagination "dissolves, diffuses, dissipates, in order to recreate: or where this process is rendered impossible, yet still . . . it struggles to idealize and unify."

This side excursion into Coleridge's and Wordsworth's and St. Thomas's concerns about the operation of mind in nature allows us to call particular attention to a distinction between imagination as a desirable and necessary action of mind in its pursuit of truth and the fancy as potentially perverse in its relation to truth. When imagination surrenders to fancy, sentiment is very likely to surrender to sentimentality. The effect of such capitulation of sovereign authority of the mind over its operations is a disorientation, that deracination of mind and spirit in the immediate world, which leaves us "Yankees of the race of men." We will then have lost that sense of place that is so pervasive of "Southernness," most particularly our individual place in the complex world. Once more, if our exploration of these matters has the validity I believe it has, we may better appreciate the recent, titillating coincidence of the *Playboy* and *Hallmark* species of sentimentality, for a fading moment much talked about. But let us recall it as comic illustration of a most serious concern.

Miss Vanessa Williams, in 1984, agonized in the public press for days over whether she should give up her title as Miss America following *Penthouse* magazine's publication of photos of her in sexually explicit poses with another woman. Among the several losses to Miss Williams was income from another photo, a demure but inviting portrait of her that was to have appeared on Kellogg's Corn Flakes boxes destined for the breakfast tables of Middle America. Thus the coincidence of sentimentalities: along with the inviting cereal portrait would have appeared that portrait of the cereal itself—the scientific analysis in a table of vitamins that promises us that the life we save by eating the product will be that of a healthy body; the "scientific" argument would be supported by visual proof in the rosebud beauty of Miss Williams taken in her prime. But then came the sudden canker to vitamins and blushing youth, the shadow cast on the morning cereal box by the morning news. The disquiet in Kellogg's advertising offices, in anticipation of public reaction, encourages me to believe that there remains at least a residual recognition by the public of impropriety. But I wonder whether, given the training in words our ad makers receive, any one of them thought how appropriate Blake's "Sick Rose" was to the situation:

O Rose thou art sick.
The invisible worm,
That flies in the night
In the howling storm:

Has found out thy bed
Of crimson joy:
And his dark secret love
Does thy life destroy.

If any of you should be inclined to send Miss Williams a late sympathy or get-well card, given such cruel treatment by the media and me, wait. The latest news, after which I turned off the event, was that she was negotiating for a guest acting role, following the ubiquitous talk-show appearances. Perhaps she did finally appear on either afternoon or prime time soap opera, on what one of our freshmen called, alas more in ignorance than in art, a "soul popper," his mishearing of "soap opera." I refrain from suggesting that some of those people possibly scandalized by Miss Williams's intrusion on their breakfast cereal boxes are likely to receive her in the living room via television, with afternoon juice or tea, though the patronage of a Phil Donahue, as revealed in surveys, rather firmly urges the conclusion.

We may see, with the help of Richard Weaver, some of the ironies resulting from our juxtaposing the two lives of Vanessa

Williams, ironies that support our contention that both portraits are distortions made possible through the decay of sentiment. In *Ideas Have Consequences,* Weaver recalls us to a known but forgotten depth in the word *obscene.* He objects that "The extremes of passion and suffering are served up to enliven the breakfast table or to lighten the boredom of an evening at home. The area of privacy has been abandoned because the definition of person has been lost. . . . Behind the offense lies the repudiation of sentiment in favor of immediacy." Weaver's objection is directed at newspaper treatment of passion, television not yet having established primacy in the perversion of sentiment. The particular instances Weaver uses seem at first far removed from our Vanessa Williams. "How common is it today," he says, "to see upon the front page of some organ destined for a hundred thousand homes the agonized face of a child run over in the street, the dying expression of a woman crushed by a subway train. . . . These are obscenities." Weaver is certainly right. And one who cannot identify an instance to illustrate Weaver's point from the current evening paper, and several from the evening television news, is not paying attention.

Let us recall that, in high Greek tragedy, as separate from routine accident, the Greeks appreciated person: in the hero, and so by extension in the passing citizen. At the height of Sophocles' play, the poet shows us the proper role of sentiment in relation to passion in the way he handles Oedipus's blinding of himself. For, though Oedipus agonizes beyond any power of words or pictures, he is made to turn to self-destruction off stage—that is, *ab-scene.* It is, properly speaking, an obscene act. Were the action presented before the audience, the audience would participate in a violation of person, as one is made to participate in such a violation in the picture of the agonized face of a child if one consents to the evening news. One who supposes Sophocles moved by deference to "Victorian" or "Puritan" Greeks in his artistic strategy does not know the Greek stomach of fifth-century Athens. He puts the event off stage in the interest of the health of sentiment in the audience as a higher end for art. It would be grossly improper to intrude upon Oedipus in such a private moment of passionate agony; the effect upon the hero himself would reduce agony to spectacle, thereby reducing both Oedipus and the audience from the moment of catharsis.[9]

To Richard Weaver's instances of the obscene treatment of accident victims by the media, let us add from our memory the unending flood made possible by the advent of television. For television's "immediacy" has long since superseded both the radio's and the newspaper's. I still recall with particular anger the repeated questions asked of bereaved parents during the Atlanta child murders a few years ago. The question, reduced to its gist—and, on one occasion which I witnessed in the "live" news coverage, a literal one—was "Could you tell our viewers what it feels like to have your little boy murdered?" The question was punctuated by a mike thrust suddenly under a mother's agony-strained face, of which the viewer was given a lingering close-up as she struggled for words. In the more recent Beirut hostage crisis, the nation and local news staffs of one network staged an obscenity whose infamy should warrant criminal action. Already privy to an impending news bulletin about a particular hostage, they set up shop in a grieving family's living room. With that vantage, they could at once show both the news announcement as seen on the family's set and the reactions of the members of the hostage's family as they first heard it. It is problematic whether the Shiite terrorists or the network and its reporters are the more guilty of violence to persons in this instance. But the literal terrorists, more than the reporters and more than the violated family, were aware of the obscenity being publicized. That is, theirs was an intention from the beginning to invade millions of homes and hold a citizenry hostage to fear and pity, which in unrelieved consort is terror. Their automatic weapons were only the proximate instrument of terror; the real weapon was the television camera, which by analogy in the war now under way through terrorism is more nearly comparable to a hydrogen bomb than to an AK-47 in its effectiveness. The terrorist promise, to an anxious and fascinated Western audience, was of a literal murder to be performed before the cameras, the obscenities of a "Happening" like *Hair* raised to a unifying moment of Western history ultimately more destructive of community than an atomic explosion.

What we see in such moments does not speak very well of our

spiritual estate. For we can only be held hostage this way through our having lost our spiritual anchor in reality; we have lost certainties beyond the moment's terror or morbid curiosity. Would that the televised family had been able to castigate the reporters on the scene, the bereaved mother of the Atlanta child hurl the microphone to the pavement. Would that we might all meditate upon Faulkner's response to a reporter as he stepped from a plane at La Guardia on his way to Stockholm: "What do you consider the decadent aspect of American life today?" a reporter asked. "It's what you're doing now, Miss. . . . It's this running people down, getting interviews and photographs just because they have done something." Or because something has been done to them.

How does such a decayed state of our being come about, a state too obvious and intrusive upon conscience to be denied or ignored—too disorienting not to be sensed in our aimlessness as a community? How may we come to terms with it, short of an angry violence of opinion directed at such "soul poppers" as the news media? I believe I know a beginning, as I believe Richard Weaver and Donald Davidson knew, to whose wisdom in this matter we must add others who have spoken reflectively of our random spirit at large in the world. Before I introduce others, however, let me return to Donald Davidson and his recollections, made in 1957, of the Fugitive-Agrarians in the 1920s and 1930s. Let us remember that Mr. Davidson in those first Lamar Lectures is looking back from this podium at which I now stand, back to the turn of our century and beyond. The world he speaks of is one almost a century removed from ours. What we may find noteworthy is that the disorientation from reality that so disturbs us now is rather a constant in human history, though it may seem overwhelmingly pervasive in this moment that is ours out of the long world's history. If we have changed newspapers and radios for televisions, it means only, so far as the evidence shows, that we have accelerated the explosion of community and family; we can hardly pretend any recovery from disintegration through such instantaneous modes of touching persons as the television news, whatever favorable arguments be given for a "global village." It may be that there are ways of approaching a fellow creature's personhood better suited to the ordering of our purported love for him than the sorts of obscenity we have seen growing out of sentimentality. Perhaps an antediluvian such as Donald Davidson may be of some help in exploring that possibility. But we will as well hold onto the realization that community is always in decay since Cain and Abel, though mayhap in accelerated conditions of decay from time to time. What one holds onto for sanity, and holds onto even with cheerfulness and good humor if "Southern," was expressed by a Yankee as he turned "Southerner." T. S. Eliot remarked that there is no such thing as a "Lost Cause" because there is no such thing as a "Gained Cause."

MR. DAVIDSON remarks the coincidence of like-minded young men at Vanderbilt just after World War I. "Our great good fortune," he says, "was that we shared pretty much the same assumptions about society, about man, nature and God. . . . It was a condition of being Southern-born. . . . There were many questions that did not need to be asked, and some of these were large metaphysical questions." He is speaking here of a convenience in that community of spirit that held the young Fugitive poets together. The large questions, particularly the metaphysical ones, very much needed asking and would be asked in due time. But Mr. Davidson is speaking of that first stage of the young men's common interest in writing poetry and appreciating the happy circumstances that fed that interest. It is in retrospect that he speaks of their pursuit of the "thankless muse," none of them at their first gatherings having had occasion to raise the angry voice of the prophet as Milton does in "Lycidas," from which Mr. Davidson takes his playful title. Increasingly, they were to become aware that their little community of poets was an island surrounded by undulating seas of indifference to poetry. Increasingly, they were to become aware that the indifferent seas eroded bonds beyond poetry; their assumptions about man, nature, and God were being steadily undercut.

Speaking from the distance of 1957, Mr. Davidson points to disturbing notes struck by those beginning poets not fully understood by them at the time. The significance and consequences of those notes began to rise in a disturbing music, whose cause would be increasingly apparent to them. There is the passage in Allen Tate's poem "To the Lacedaemonians":

> When I was a boy, the light upon the hills
> Was there because I could see it, not because
> Some special gift of God had put it there.

This is a reflection of Tate's awakening to those undulating, isolating waters we spoke of; the passage echoes, with significant differences, passages one might cite in William Wordsworth, particularly lines from *The Prelude* or, for our convenience in limiting discourse, from "Lines Composed a Few Miles above Tintern Abbey." The difference between Tate's and Wordsworth's senses of isolation is signalled by the ready and still reasonably comfortable use of the word *God* in Tate's lines. Wordsworth, more immediately awash in eighteenth-century rationalism, tries to be empirical in measuring his memory of past experience against a present experience, introducing not only images that stir feeling but data to certify image. But nowhere will he introduce such a word as *God.* The concern at issue in "Tintern Abbey" is of course that dissociation of sensibility which Eliot would make a popular critical term. Wordsworth first thought to call his poem an elegy. As such, it is a memorial to lost feeling; it seeks solace from the loss of feeling through a reconciliation with thought; thought seems not only to survive feeling but to supersede it. But in measuring a memory of past experience against a present moment of experience, Wordsworth finds no unshakable reason to accept the givenness of existence in nature. He asserts an acceptance, on faith we must conclude, and in lines that will come to haunt him: "Nature never did betray the heart that loved her." This line is in a poem which shies away from questions of evil and of death.

Tate's lines, and Wordsworth's, touch a common experience that is increasingly in the foreground of our poetry since the Renaissance. But Tate has an advantage over Wordsworth in dealing with the experience; he operates out of an ancient tradition more immediately available to him than it seems to have been to Wordsworth, though Tate may not yet have fully recognized his advantage in being "Southern-born." William of Ockham, Descartes, Locke, and a host of others had thrown spanners into the comfortable workings of mind with nature and with an immediacy of effect upon Wordsworth that had not occurred so pervasively in that "Southernness" Tate inherited. Or perhaps it is more accurate to say, the effects had not become so apparent to Tate as to Wordsworth: when he comes to write "Our Cousin, Mr. Poe" much later, Tate will have recognized disturbing intellectual elements present in the nineteenth-century South. Though a disruption of mind and nature is a problem common in the Western mind since the Renaissance, Wordsworth cannot be certain that it is indeed common. A separation of mind and nature for him had seemed so decisive that he feared as well the separation of mind from mind. What words may I use as poet which will not only engage the existing world but engage minds other than my own as well? How could Wordsworth serve as vatic poet? That he confronts the problem with heroic, if sometimes dogged, determination makes him a most valuable prophetic poet to us.

But though speaking for and to our commonality, Wordsworth nevertheless speaks often as one separated from it. It is not so much that he is given to a divine aloofness, as Keats charges, but that he struggles with his isolation at the level of his own mind, even when he asserts that the poet is a man speaking to men. His sense of isolation is out of our continuing problem with the question of the relation of consciousness to the object of which it is conscious. Biographical data concerning Wordsworth's preference for country life over city life obscures the more profound personal dimension of his poetry. There is no great English poet whose personal life is more intimately a circumstance of his poetry than Wordsworth's. But it is the personal at the level of philosophical questions bordering on the theological realm that makes Wordsworth the great poet he is. It is an over-simplification, then, to engage him as a "nature poet"—a sort of early English "Agrarian"—as is often done, a realization Eliot came to rather late. For having at first rejected Wordsworth, Eliot came to embrace him, by which point Eliot recognized that one may be more isolated in the teeming city of Paris or London than alone at Dove Cottage.

At any rate, Wordsworth, at a private remove, nevertheless has a sense of something deeply interfused in creation, including even the man-made city of London; that "something" binds all creation, including individual minds. But that is not an experience easily shared with others. Even the literal presence of Dorothy on the occasion of "Lines Composed a Few Miles above Tintern Abbey" comes as a surprise to the reader late in the poem, and one suspects it is almost as much a surprise to the speaker of the poem, rather certainly Wordsworth, who has been so caught up with the problem of his consciousness in relation to all creation separate from consciousness as to have forgotten her presence. Wordsworth reaches for the binding "something in nature," though giving it no traditional name, in an attempt to certify his own existence.

If a term like *God* at first comes easily into Fugitive poetry, the Fugitives were nevertheless beginning to engage metaphysical questions to justify its presence as more than the inherited shibboleth that Wordsworth tried to avoid. It must have been a shock to the liberated intelligentsia of 1919 that John Crowe Ransom called his first collection *Poems About God.* The title at the time might well seem to them to border upon a display of bad manners. But then, there was a sufficiently conspicuous presence in those poems, a new use of old prosody, that he couldn't quite be ignored. What was one to make of such a phenomenon? It is always easier in retrospect, after we have arrived at certain ends, to see patterns pointing toward those ends. We traditionalists are always insistently urging the importance of history to our thinking on these very grounds, in the hope that such patterns perceived in the past and touching the present may become a present means of anticipating future contingencies. Isolated minds, among them these young Vanderbilt poets, were becoming concerned with relationships among the creatures of creation, concerned with the patterns in words whereby those relationships may be explored, certified, embraced, and justified. The Imagists had, in a dead-end practice of naturalism, settled upon nouns and adjectives as central to their attempt to hold a mirror up to particular objects in nature; they abandoned not only formal prosody as a rule, but the formalities of syntax that make adjectives and nouns significant to our discursive minds. In doing so, they turned away from the complexities of existence, from the resonances of analogy to, at their best, metaphor as mirror, even as they professed the more strongly that through art they embraced reality.

The Imagists' problematic attempt is one form of a distortion which Mr. Davidson talks about in his poem "The Ninth Part of Speech," a poem he sets first in his collected poems. In school, the poem says, words and symbols, which settle rather often in nouns and their adjectives (see Heidegger) unsettle the mind with "Problems that flare out like a comet's tail, / Unsolved equations, surded with bane and bale." Those problems must at last be confronted, so that mind through its symbols may be reconciled to the reality that flares up through symbol with such disturbing effect upon mind. One uses the eight parts of speech, not just nouns and adjectives. But there is that ninth part, without which the eight are all helpless because merely empty vessels undipped in being. We

> Must move beyond a printed grammar's reach
> And try some parleying among birch boughs
> With beaver, deer, and the neat scurrying grouse
> Who use what is their own.

Let us be certain we understand Davidson. Otherwise we will confuse him with the early Wordsworth, who addresses to us a principle of education at first sight like Davidson's. Wordsworth advises us to "quit" our books and "Let Nature be [our] teacher." The emphasis in Wordsworth is on an immediacy of mind to nature that is possible when one abandons books, when one abandons—if taken literally—that most direct presence of remote history to our being. It is here that Wordsworth is most "modern." (Left suspended is the question why he should himself be so heavily dependent upon tradition, upon freighted language.) But Davidson's is an elegy written in an abandoned Tennessee schoolhouse, not under a dark sycamore in the south England countryside. His lament?

> Few now are left who know the ancient rule
> That tame abstract must wed the wild particular
> In school or art, but most of all in school,
> Else learning's spent to gild a fool
> At market, altar, bench, or bar.

We know Mr. Davidson too sophisticated a student of English poetry to doubt the deliberate echo of Wordsworth and a correction of the Wordsworthean, neo-Rousseauistic educational program. It was too excessive a program, even for Wordsworth, of course. If Wordsworth invokes Milton in a ringing sonnet against the corruptions of England's "fireside, sword, and pen," it is not only Milton of the moral conscience, but Milton the last Renaissance man—full of learning and of worldly activity, but most of all of learning. Indeed, so prodigious a mind that Eliot will presently tax Milton as one of the agents who helped separate thought from feeling.[10]

For Davidson, the parleying with beaver, deer, and grouse—to which we have added possum—makes it possible to move toward incarnating the abstract, thus anchoring mind in creation. We recall Flannery O'Connor's description of fiction as an "incarnational art," by which she means very nearly what Davidson does. But even more decisively, let us recall St. Thomas's argument that form in the mind actualizes mind, that there is a mutual service between mind and nature initiated by the mind's "in-forming" itself from nature. That is the service to mind of that ninth part of speech, in an educational primer of mind that prepares one to recognize the Cause of creation through the logical form of creation itself.[11]

But that poem is ahead for Davidson. Before it can be written, the Fugitives must, by the labor of mind, justify an order inherited by birth. In his early poems, Tate speaks also of language. In "Causerie," he was becoming disturbed by a variance within his own speech about such matters as God and Nature, and by the encroaching speech of commercially advancing Nashville. He had for a while found comfortable haven in a shared language at those Saturday evening Fugitive gatherings at Sidney Hirsch's. The larger world, however, increasingly intruded, raising a question that had to be dealt with:

> What is this conversation, now secular,
> A speech not mine yet speaking for me in
> The heaving jelly of my tribal air?

What Tate and his fellows found increasingly destructive were those voices which spoke "Southern" about matters "Southern" but with a perspective in the voices decidedly foreign to the young poets' understanding of "Southernness." As Davidson will later argue in dealing with "Mr. Cash and the Proto-Dorian South," Cash argued for "*the* Southern mind, not *a* Southern mind or *some* Southern minds." The Dorian invaders, with their Spartan activism, were threatening to appropriate "Southernness" to ends some "Southerners" could not accept. Just how subtly managed the appropriation, given the decay of the *ratio* through that specialization of intellect called science and an ascendancy from sentiment into sentimentality, Davidson had already attacked. In his poem "On a Replica of the Parthenon," he castigates the New Spartan's appropriation of old Athens by a conquest of "Southern" spirit.

> Why do they come? What do they seek
> Who build but never read their Greek?

The loss of the venerable is mocked by the modernist pretense of remembrance, the replica of the Parthenon. (I hear ads even now directed at country music fans, inviting them to tour Nashville landmarks—visit the replica of the Parthenon and Conway Twitty's swimming pool made in the shape of a guitar.) Thus sentiment becomes sentimentality, Davidson suggests. The change is reflected by the shopgirls on lunch break who

> embrace a plaster thought,
> And eye Poseidon's loins ungirt,
> And never heed the brandished spear
> Or feel the bright-eyed maiden's rage
> Whose gaze the sparrows violate.

Poseidon or Athene provide resting points for a moment disengaged from nature and history. The shopgirls' eyes are arrested; in combination, the restlessly perching sparrows whose droppings glaze the eyes in the figure of Athene: these details suggest Davidson might have called his poem "Shopgirls among the Sparrows." The poem concludes more directly than Eliot's Sweeney poem:

> Pursue not wisdom or virtue here,
> But what blind motion, what dim last
> Regret of men who slew their past
> Raised up this bribe against their fate.

Little wonder that the Fugitives were increasingly concerned with that "blind motion" in their "Southern" fellows, the effect of which motion was to reduce regional men to provincial men. Tate will also look back upon that moment, in what is now a classical distinction between the regional, which he praises, and the provincial, already characterized by him as the "heaving jelly" of our "tribal air." To understand the blind motion in us, says Tate in his essay "The New Provincialism," we must make this distinction:

> Regionalism is . . . limited in space but not in time. The provincial attitude is limited in time but not in space. . . . provincialism is that state of mind in which regional men lose their origin in the past and its continuity into the present, and begin every day as if there had been no yesterday. . . . what a difference—and it is a difference between two worlds: the provincial world of the present, which sees in material welfare and legal justice the whole solution to the human problem; and the classical-Christian world, based upon regional consciousness, which held that honor, truth, imagination, human dignity, and limited acquisitiveness, could alone justify a social order however rich and efficient it may be. . . . From now on we are committed to seeing *with,* not *through* the eye: we, as provincials who do not live anywhere.

Those words Tate wrote at the end of World War II, his theme a dominant one in Davidson's Lamar Lectures a decade later. Mr. Davidson explores the deepening concern of the young Fugitives with the provincial cancer eating away at the regional spirit. The effects of that canker of spirit might be discovered symptomatically in shopgirls looking at a Greek hero's private parts, oblivious of the whole, and especially of the brandished spear which promises a violent if unexpected cost to such plastic thought raised against our past. (One is reminded here of Andrew Lytle's title essay, "The Hero with the Private Parts.")

A destructive vision comes in the melding of the eight parts of speech with the ninth, and is unlikely to come without all in concert, given that we are rational creatures—discursive animals at the least. If we abandon the dimension of mind enlarged by vision, of which grammar is symbolic, and instead pursue a provincial spatiality, a conquest of the surface of being with our plaster thought, we shall not merely be rejecting history as we pursue the chimera of progress, for the future is future history also. Most destructively, we shall thereby reject our individual potential being. I do not mean to suggest that history alone is the heal-all for individual or community health. It is but a complex of broadening trails as it approaches the present moment; that is one aspect to be seriously recognized of it. It is but part of our larger inheritance through the actuality of our being in time, as our bodily nature is another. Insofar as we may suitably rescue history, it will not then be through raising replicas of time past in static museums of the mind. Such a rescue, certainly, would not answer Mr. Tate's question about the "light upon the hills," as if time past, brought thus into the present, were an adequate end to our pursuit of fulfillment either as individual or community. Indeed, what we will discover is that there are various ways whereby we may entrap ourselves in time; we can do so by embracing history in the wrong way no less than by rejecting it altogether. The uses of historiography, rising in the eighteenth century as a gnostic instrument, encourage one to such violation of history. The more popular rejection of history altogether, while it does not directly subvert history to gnostic restructurings of being, nevertheless leaves us facing the present moment always from an *ad hoc* necessity with an unformed intellect. Such a mind is most susceptible to the maneuvers of gnosticism. (The mind content to reject history is seldom likely to stop there, rejecting much else as well, especially art.)

Through history, we may indeed be tempted to turn back the clock, leaving ourselves an ineffectual being such as E. A. Robinson's Miniver Cheevy. Yet without history, we are left rather in the position of stopping the clock altogether, or speeding it up in such ways that seconds, minutes, hours no longer signify by analogy those logical, seasonal dimensions in nature itself. Either way, fancy will have disconnected thought from reality. When one of our National "fathers" complains that "Our age is retrospective. It builds sepulchres of the fathers," the answer is that some do, alas. But when he adds, "Why should we grope among the dry bones of the past," his rhetorical question implying a rejection of history, we should recognize him as one of our false fathers, though we have institutionalized sepulchres to him for over a hundred years on the basis of precisely such advice to ignore the past. (The father spoken of here is, of course, Emerson.) One has established his being not at all when he rejects that haunting Eden of the past, the trail from which leads inescapably into the present moment, in favor of any dream Eden, whose secret cause is the gnostic restructuring of being whereby one man struggles to be the primary dreammaker.

The Fugitives in their Agrarian stage were engaging such questions as we are here raising, particularly that question of questions concerning the intersection of time by the timeless, the mystery through which times past, present, and future are annealed so that we may turn from lamenting an Eden lost and not at once be trapped by dreams of Edens yet to be. The young Fugitives had already made a break of sorts with a regional history reduced to a lament for Eden. In the initial issue of their magazine they declared: "Official exception having been taken by the sovereign people to the mint julep, a literary phase known rather euphemistically as Southern Literature has expired, like any other stream whose source is stopped up."

If there was a certain bravado in such posturing that would later embarrass Mr. Davidson, the young poets nevertheless recognized a sense in which history could be a dead hand of the past. History so used could only enlarge the authority of those who would reject history altogether. Already they were working at histories and biographies, sorting out and assimilating the ways in which history must be taken if its uses and comforts are to be valid beyond food for nostalgia or a toolchest for the remaking of existence to conform to dream blueprints. For they had recognized the most immediate and deadly enemy to individual and community life to be that modernist mind which refuses such distinctions.

That enemy has come to be named rather widely as secular gnosticism in our day, a term I have been using. The name emerges through the revisiting of the past by a number of important modern thinkers, the most influential of whom is Eric Voegelin. His work was getting under way in Europe and moving in a direction parallel to that of the Fugitives as they themselves became increasingly aware of their prophetic calling as poets. Now secular gnosticism in its first attempt upon the popular mind, which it is concerned to restructure, recognized the importance of separating nature from grace in that mind. Nature divested of grace loses numen for that distorted mind. Such a mind may then the more easily accept nature as a prime matter with which to build gnostic dream life, whatever the dream's particular delineation. It matters little to such a mind, short of its sudden recognition of grace in creation, if one insist that such restructuring is always doomed by the inevitable intrusion of reality upon the dream, by that inescapable *thisness* of existence that lies deeper in being than our manipulations of surfaces.[12]

But my enthusiasm for pattern seen in retrospect has moved my argument too quickly beyond the young Fugitives. Between the cessation of *The Fugitive* and the publication of *I'll Take My Stand,* questions long festering in their poetry became insistent. By what pursuit could these young compatriots, and the enlarging company of like-minded historians and economists they came to know, pursue the gnawing questions? Tate, in his "Horatian Epode to the Duchess of Malfi," says a way that suits the poet. The speaker of the poem finds himself standing in two worlds most uncomfortably, in consequence of having been forced to "considerations of the void" which sees death as splitting "the straight line of pessimism / Into two infinities." From that point of view, he must conclude that

> It is moot whether there be divinities
> As I finish this play by Webster. . . .
> The catharsis fades in the warm water of a yawn.

Thus the provincial mind dramatized by Tate's speaker, possessed of that modernist virtue, ennui. But that speaker had set out as regional mind, and the mode of regional address is signalled as the poem begins in a sentence set off in parentheses, almost as an aside; perhaps it is more nearly an assertion by our poet than by the speaker of the poem, a statement the most-often quoted of all Tate's work. The words are: "the form requires the myth." In this light, the replica of the Parthenon is form without myth.

We ought to note that the poem here quoted appears in the

second number of the first volume of *Fugitive* in October 1922. That is the very same month and year in which another American fugitive poet, having fled Emerson's Harvard for London, published an arresting poem in another little magazine. His is a poem which has reordered our concerns with literature since its appearance. I mean, of course, *The Waste Land,* which Eliot published in the first issue of his own little magazine, *The Criterion.* Let me suggest that Tate and Davidson and Ransom and Warren were in significant ways already beyond the concerns that brought Eliot to compose his poem. If we look at Eliot's review of James Joyce's *Ulysses* in *The Dial* (November 1923), we hear him saying of myth in relation to art: "[Using myth] is simply a way of controlling, of ordering, of giving a shape and significance to the immense panorama of futility and anarchy which is contemporary history. . . . Instead of the narrative method, we may now use the mythical method. It is, I believe, a step toward making a modern world possible for art." This approach to myth is decidedly different from one which says that the form requires the myth. Eliot had not yet reached that comfortable spiritual and intellectual position he would later dramatize in "Ash-Wednesday," when for him myth's relation to form anchored form at last in one's belief in myth—anchored form in the nature of creation and so in the implications that creation is in somewise a caused being. But at the time of *The Waste Land,* Eliot's words suggest, myth was for him an instrument through which he might establish a private sanity in the midst of the general chaos of modern history; underneath that chaos seemed to lie the void, considerations of which were insistently voiced by both science and philosophy.

If John Crowe Ransom in the early 1920s found form inadequate in Eliot's poetry, arguing against Tate's defense of Eliot, Davidson demurred also. But Davidson's disquiet lay rather with Eliot's attempt to use myth in the interest of what seemed a merely aesthetic order. Such an abuse of myth, for Davidson, reduces myth to the level of an instrument in the employ of intellect; it serves the personal convenience of the poet, separate from any truth beyond private convenience. It does not recognize myth's relation to the reality of creation. I believe Mr. Davidson misunderstands to a degree Eliot's actual use of myth in his poem; he seems to take it that Eliot shared the intellectual attitude of Sir James Frazer and Jessie Weston toward myth, rationalizing it as merely residual history—seeing myth as the attempt by less advanced people than ourselves to understand the course of nature in time. One needs to note, however, what Eliot says in his notes. He pays a very careful tribute to Weston's recent book *From Ritual to Romance.* The title, plan, and "a good deal of the incidental symbolism" of his poem were suggested by the book. Her work will "elucidate" some of the difficulties in the poem. But this is far from being an endorsement of Weston's own intellectual attitude toward myth. So too will St. Augustine's *Confessions* elucidate the poem; if a less specific source for parallels throughout *The Waste Land,* Augustine's *Confessions* is most crucial at the climactic point, at which juncture Frazer and Weston and similar modernist sensibilities that seem to have dominated the first three hundred lines are being left behind: "to Carthage then I came." Deeper recognitions of origins and ends intrude progressively. I mean only to suggest that Eliot's uses of and his tribute to the new sociological anthropology of Frazer and Weston do not mean he shares intellectual conclusions with the authors about the meaning of myth. Still, Davidson has a point, in that Eliot is reluctant to make any public commitment to myth beyond its being "a way" to order and shape the present anarchy of history. The poem seen retrospectively—that is, in relation to "Ash-Wednesday" and *Four Quartets*—suggests Eliot rather used by myth than using it. And his "nervous breakdown" that precedes the poem suggests that his condition of agitated nerves was a symptom of a deeper problem, his spiritual turmoil.

DAVIDSON'S RESPONSE to *The Waste Land* was his own long poem, *The Tall Men.* It incorporates the heroic spirit of Western man, reaching back to Homer and moving forward through Virgil, into the Anglo-Saxon world, on through the North American settlements, coming down to the Nashville of the poet's own day. It is a poem differing widely from Eliot's and Joyce's allusive and indirect manner, intending rather to emphasize a continuity to be treasured and enlivened. There is for Davidson a heroic succession in history whose analogue is the apostolic succession in history.

I introduce the analogy deliberately. Eliot delivered the Page-Barbour Lectures at the University of Virginia, published under the title *After Strange Gods: A Primer of Modern Heresy* in 1933. Although he doesn't include himself—that is, the early Eliot—as heretic, he does begin the lectures by acknowledging that the problem he addressed in "Tradition and the Individual Talent" (1919) "does not seem to me so simple as it seemed then, nor can I treat it now as a purely literary one." It follows, of course, that he would be unable to treat such a concern as the "dissociation of sensibilities," introduced into our critical awareness in 1921, as a purely literary problem either. And one of the reasons he could not he speaks of immediately in his second paragraph, the recent appearance of *I'll Take My Stand,* to which he pays a somewhat cautious tribute, discussing at some length his recent observations of geographical differences, North and South, and the reflections of native character revealed in landscapes as molded by persons in Virginia and New England. He speaks now, not as New Englander, but as British subject when he says he feels that "the chances for the re-establishing of a native culture are better here [in Virginia and the South] than in New England," and for reasons suggested by the Twelve Southerners. These reflections he will also address in verse in a series of slight poems, "Landscapes," whose common presence is a restless spirit seeking accommodation to place.

In the first of these landscapes, "New Hampshire," the "Children's voices in the orchard" move the speaker back twenty years, but the speaker concludes that "the spring is over." In the second, "Virginia," the speaker brings with him "Ever moving / Iron thoughts" and takes them away as he goes, unable to settle comfortably among the purple and white trees with their delay and decay that seem to reflect a temperament in Southern character not comfortably amenable. This is an old remembrance of New England character, one which Eliot introduced earlier in "Gerontion" and directly out of Henry Adams's own boyhood encounter with Virginia landscape along the Potomac, that encounter in "depraved May," of "dogwood and chestnut, flowering judas." The final of Eliot's landscapes, "Cape Ann," returns to childhood's rich remembrance of life on that northern shoreline, but the speaker must "resign this land at the end. . . . The palaver is finished." Not quite finished, of course, since he will engage "our first world" of the rose garden, where "the leaves were full of children" in *Burnt Norton* and begin that reconciliation which is far advanced in "Ash-Wednesday" and concerns him so explicitly in *After Strange Gods*.

What Eliot is preparing for in his opening remarks of the lectures by the introduction of the Fugitive-Agrarians and his response to the American landscape, North and South, is an elaboration of a distinction between *tradition* and *orthodoxy.* He will presently say in the lectures

> that a *tradition* is rather a way of feeling and acting which characterizes a group throughout generations; . . . it must largely be . . . unconscious; whereas the maintenance of *orthodoxy* is a matter which calls for the exercise of all our conscious intelligence. . . . Tradition has not the means to criticize itself. . . . And while tradition, being a matter of good habits, is necessarily real only in a social group, orthodoxy exists whether realised in anyone's thought or not. Orthodoxy also, of course represents a consensus between the living and the dead. . . . Tradition may be conceived as a by-product of right living, not to be aimed at directly. It is of the blood, so to speak, rather than of the brain.

Given this distinction in relation to what Eliot says in the small poems and about American landscape in the lectures, one might well conclude that Eliot now sees tradition as a social conditioning, actually very like the conditioning of a child by nature that he remembers and elegizes in almost Wordsworthean mode in the "Landscapes." It is as if to argue that through tradition we remain at a natural level until tradition is baptized by "the exercise of all our conscious intelligence." But there is one "baptism" of tradition by intellect whose result is not orthodox, that whereby tradition is a willed appropriation of the past into the present. That rather seems Eliot's earlier understanding of the uses of myth in ordering poetry, and although there is no evidence in his setting aside of that understanding in his lectures that he has Davidson directly in mind, it shows a recognition of the point Davidson objects to in the Eliot of "Tradition and the Individual Talent" and of *The Waste Land.* For there is a personal truth to Eliot's later characterization of *The Waste Land* as "a personal grouse."

The point of our attention to *After Strange Gods* is to suggest that for the Fugitive-Agrarians, and especially for Davidson and Tate, there is an orthodoxy in tradition itself, requiring the intellect's discovery of a validity in tradition deeper than merely its presence "in a social group." To have been "Southern-born" was to have had a laying on of hands by tradition as it were, a touching of both heart and mind affecting both blood and brain. To sort out and recover to active life that tradition required the services of not only "all our conscious intelligence," but the authority of heart as a corrective to those manipulations of tradition which conscious intelligence is capable of, even in the name of orthodoxy. That manipulation of history dries the stream of history, leaving residually mint juleps and hoop skirts. The dangers of setting aside the blood's tradition as incapable of criticizing itself is that one grants rational, conscious intellect an authority which easily leads it to gnostic heresy. That is, I suggest, precisely the difficulty in that most fascinating and difficult of our traditionalists, Ezra Pound, the history of whose life and the art of whose poetry I believe substantiate the suggestion. For if Eliot found himself unable to accept tradition as it had at first appeared to be to him, the traditionalist seen as one who appropriated myth to "use" in the present moment, Pound seldom gives evidence of disquiet with that procedure. (One could, I believe, make profitable study of this difference by exploring Pound's *Cantos* in relation to David Jones's *Anathemata.*)

It is this danger in the manipulation of tradition that prompts Davidson to write his *Tall Men* in the mode he chooses, the narrative rather than the mythical, in Eliot's distinction of the modes. Joyce's uses of the *Odyssey* as a complicating backdrop to Bloom's day, or Eliot's juxtaposition of Sweeney and Agamemnon, among other effects, emphasize the gulf between the modern and ancient worlds, the "mythical" presence of the ancient serving as counterpoint to a primary interest in the order of the art itself. I take this to be the point Eliot intends in his comment on Joyce's novel, and by implication on his own great poem, when he says that "the narrative method" is now superseded by "the mythical method." In this respect, there is considerable justice in William Carlos Williams's angry response that Eliot through *The Waste Land* managed to return poetry to the authority of the academy.[13]

Davidson deliberately chooses the "narrative method," not simply to order his work of art, but to order it in relation to its historical materials so that he might reveal a continuity, the "heroic succession" we spoke of. He reveals in the present moment of the speaking voice of his poem vital presences in that voice of a sequential tradition; the recognitions thus recovered would justify the speaker's existence in the modern world as a member of what Eliot calls in his Page-Barbour Lectures "a group throughout generations." The voice of orthodoxy might phrase it a community in tune. It is in recognition of membership in that community that Davidson's speaker makes legitimate his oppositions to the contrary gnostic forces. I think one might put it that Davidson's poem is quite deliberately that of a prophetic poet, while Eliot's *Waste Land* shows its poet to be in quest of a prophetic voice, a voice that emerges in his later poems. To make such a comparison in no wise makes a critical judgment as to which is the greater poem, a concern which would first have to examine each poem in respect to what it is attempting to be: the narrative method and the mythical method exert aesthetic pressures differing from each other no doubt; there is the obvious complication as well that the modes are not mutually exclusive within either of the poems taken separately. A poem in itself implies the conditions of its perfections, though juxtaposing perfections in analogous poems is often helpful. But we are not concerned at this point to determine just how faithfully each poet is committed to the good of the thing made, a most legitimate and inviting concern. We are rather concerned here with the general intellectual and spiritual climate of the 1920s within which each poet worked and with his response to that climate. And a part of that climate for Davidson (as it was for William Carlos Williams) was the growing presence of that poem called *The Waste*

Land. In objecting to what appeared an absence of piety toward myth's validity, Davidson dramatizes his retrospection of the heroic tradition, moving from Homer's day down to Nashville, Tennessee, in the 1920s. He believes the spirit he celebrates is still alive, in spite of our nervously raising bribes against our fate, in which actions stir superstitions within the modern mind about its history. For it is a form of superstition to raise monuments to unknown forces, such bribes of Fate as that replica of the Parthenon. There is for Davidson too much similarity, perhaps, between the facile juxtaposition of Nashville's progressivist spirit to Greek civilization and the ironic yoking of Leopold Bloom and Odysseus or Sweeney and Agamemnon.

It was as if Davidson wished to show in his own poem that myth forms a deeper and more constant stream in the affairs of man than any modern restrictions upon it as merely "fiction" can erase. Myth as fiction is a deconstruction of the meaning of myth which we owe to Renaissance appropriations of the Greek and Roman worlds, as Mircea Eliade would later point out in *Myth and Reality* (1963). That an abuse of myth was indeed Davidson's objection is reflected in a letter he wrote the editor of the *Georgia Review* shortly after an essay highly critical of John Stewart's book on the Fugitive-Agrarians appeared in the *Review.* This essay was my own "Bells for John Stewart's *Burden,*" and I hope I may be pardoned for quoting the letter, since it does give added authority to my comments on *The Tall Men.* Mr. Davidson says of my essay,

> At various points Montgomery makes good use of the comparison between T. S. Eliot ("The Wasteland") and the Fugitive-Agrarians. I'm much pleased to have The Tall Men discussed in this connection. Montgomery must be the first critic to notice that that book is in some measure a counterpart to Eliot's negativity. It was so intended—but who was I to oppose, even indirectly, the author of the Sweeney poems, the Sacred Wood, etc., etc., to say nothing of the "Wasteland"? It is true, of course, that in opposing I *learned* something from T. S. E.

While rejecting Eliot's "negativity," he also recognizes in such works as the Sweeney poems and *The Sacred Wood* Eliot's own version of shopgirls juxtaposed to Athene and Poseidon.

There are interesting coincidences wherever we struggle for order, coincidences which we may take as accidental or random and therefore attempt to categorize with that catchall mode of laying difficult question or separating ourselves from it; namely, the mode of irony. One may say, then, that there is an irony in Mr. Davidson's having published his *Tall Men* the same year Eliot published "Ash-Wednesday," by which time Eliot is more openly pious in his address to myth. He is at that point, in fact, much closer to Mr. Davidson's position than the Nashville poet had yet had opportunity to recognize. The more interesting question, however, is why such different minds, so widely removed from each other by their personal histories, should so largely coincide on important concerns for myth in relation to history? Eliot becomes, as Davidson already was, an advocate for the recovery of the spiritual to a modernist, secular climate. Undoubtedly, the agency of grace is one answer which neither poet would reject. As for the means of that grace in operation, I think it rather likely to have been for one of them (Eliot) an intrusion of reality upon intellectualized illusions; for the other (Davidson) it was rather the development of a rational understanding of his sentiment, alive in him by virtue of his being "Southern-born." It is conspicuous in Eliot that he is, for most of his life, uncomfortable with having been New England–born, though literally born on the border of North and South in St. Louis. (He recognizes his borderland situation, sometimes directly articulating it.) But in relation to his Unitarian *née* Puritan family origins and his intellectual training at that institution of secularized Puritanism, Charles W. Eliot's Harvard, Eliot was left hard-pressed to discover any meaning to existence. That led him on a desperate and immediate philosophical journey in pursuit of some link between consciousness and the objects of consciousness—to the study of phenomenology, and specifically to a doctoral study of F. H. Bradley; concomitant to that study are those early poems that demonstrate my argument, especially his "Preludes" and "The Love Song of J. Alfred Prufrock."

Davidson, on the other hand, had a less difficult journey to make, although he, too, could not escape encounter with those large metaphysical questions. He had, as he thankfully recognizes, inherited a community of understanding about man, nature, and God less desperately engaged than by New England intellectualism such as Eliot's. Davidson's problem was not to come to, but to advance and justify that intimacy between man and nature in their relation to God which was already his by inheritance. From Davidson's point of view, Eliot seen from some distance—through his public address to myth, for instance—proved helpful to the exploration of myth's validity.

Before *The Waste Land* came to disturb the Nashville coterie, however, the young Fugitives were already embattled with contemporary manifestations of "modern" poetry. The loss of an ordinate role between form and myth is disturbing to the degree it forces one to consider whether, in such a divided world as that already conspicuous at Vanderbilt and in Nashville, "It is moot" that divinities exist, as Tate says in his "Horatian Epode." The causes of that dissociation of sensibilities which troubled Eliot—the separation of thought and feeling, with the subsequent effects of that separation upon English poetry—were pursued by the Fugitives back beyond Eliot's culprits in Milton's and Dryden's age. But it will remain for Richard Weaver, whom we may properly call a second-generation Fugitive-Agrarian, to put the telling word upon the point of dissociation. In *Ideas Have Consequences,* Weaver names William of Ockham as the agent of that infection of Western thought which we have already had occasion to speak of, namely Nominalism. It was Ockham "who propounded the fateful doctrine of nominalism, which denies that universals have a real existence. The practical result of nominalist philosophy is to banish the reality which is perceived by the intellect and to posit as reality that which is perceived by the senses." Such a dissociation will inevitably lead to Sweeneys or to characters like Hazel Motes in *Wise Blood.* Haze, for instance, is most insistent that only what the senses perceive is to be believed. We must not overlook here that Ockham finds his principal enemy to be St. Thomas Aquinas, who is insistent that through the senses we draw closer to what Weaver calls universals with real existence; most particularly, Thomas means God as the supremely real reality who gives reality to universals no less than to particular manifestations. Consequently, the ideas we have about things sensual and ideas about universals are crucially related to each other. And that means that the names we give things have to be understood as judging us by the very act of our giving the names. Names, then, are not arbitrary, as we suggested earlier in recalling Adams's ritual of naming in the Garden. All nine parts of speech go together in an approach to that one great word, that Yes, that I AM THAT I AM which is the absolute anchor of imagination for the poet. That one word which man has struggled to say from the beginning is the most important action possible to his intellect. When nominalism, then, introduces the principle that naming is an arbitrary act of mind, that names are inconsequential to reality except as convenience, that the only reality is that of the senses, then the liberties we take with reality in the interest of power over reality proliferate. We enter an age which Eric Voegelin calls Modern Gnosticism, in which that complex of disintegrations of spirit occurred that we have been talking about all along in defining *obscenity, sentiment, sentimentality, idea*. In each instance, we have rather stressed that there is a relation between the word we give a thing and its reality, a relation to be ignored at the cost of spiritual chaos in each person and in family and community. And that is why the good "Southerner," who is by intuition an antinominalist, will begin his recipe, "First, catch a possum." He means that we must start with that "little white beast," whether in so insisting he is a "Southerner" such as St. Thomas Aquinas in the *Summa Theologiae* or a Donald Davidson in "The Ninth Part of Speech."

Three

POSSUM, POSSE, POTUI

WHATEVER the place or time in which the fearful malady of the soul occurs—that dissociation of sensibilities—it marks consequentially the particular soul in which it occurs. It affects our bearing in the world; it is imprinted in and by our gestures, so that we at once reveal our divided self and, unfortunately, sometimes affect the world beyond us by our distorted gestures. And so it is in the language of the new poetry about them in the 1920s that the Fugitives became increasingly aware of disjunction in the souls of poets. It seemed to the young men of Nashville, as Davidson was to put it in the first of his Lamar Lectures, that "Either [the new poets] were caught up in the superficial excitement that attended the 'New Poetry' and practiced facile imitation of its merely rhetorical features . . . or else they were imitating the rhetoric of nineteenth century poetry without any question as to its promises."

In what he says of this "New Poetry," one has a hint of his old dissatisfaction with the early Eliot. Davidson's objections to the "merely rhetorical features" of that poetry is a charge in effect that the poet is a sophist, lacking that piety toward the world whose consequence is a piety toward language as well, so that the grounding of the eight parts of speech reflects a fundamental engagement of that ninth part. There is evidence in the poetry itself, within "a printed grammar's reach," whether or not that necessary "parleying" with deer and grouse and possum has occurred. For that reason, a sophistical, disconnected poetry is a betrayal of the academy itself.[1]

As for those sentimentalist poets still echoing the nineteenth century, the Fugitives (says Davidson) "could not grant that Tennyson and Browning, or nineteenth century poetry in general, offered very sound examples of the application of the formal element of poetry. We turned back to Shakespeare and Milton." And, under Tate's urging, to Baudelaire and the French Symbolists, as both Pound and Eliot had done. Among their older contemporaries, the Fugitives found that only Hardy and Yeats held their respect, a respect these poets (Yeats and Hardy) continued to hold as witnessed by Ransom's lifelong commitment to Hardy and Davidson's steady offering at Vanderbilt of a course in Yeats—and Eliot.

One notices in these quotations from Davidson's Lamar Lectures that he uses the terms *rhetoric* and *rhetorical* in a pejorative sense, for which reason he will subsequently clarify a proper sense of the term by quoting from an essay by Tate. But here he is concerned with rhetoric as gimmick, with a use of grammar and logic to impose fancy's form rather than submit to the labor of discovering intrinsic form in the poem. Suitable form requires a use of words that reflects the reality of things to which language has reference as conceptual origin, its anchor in a "ninth part of speech." In discovering form intrinsic to nature, poetry must be an imitation of nature's formal actions, even as St. Thomas argues. Of course, Thomas is not so very immediate in the Fugitives' thought, certainly not in the way he is directly familiar to those artists awakened by Maritain's *Art and Scholasticism* or Gilby's *Poetic Experience*—such poets and artists as David Jones, Eric Gill, and Flannery O'Connor. Maritain's book would not be readily available till the year *I'll Take My Stand* was published and Gilby's not till 1934. Nevertheless, what was occurring among the Fugitives was a native discovery of truths about art which had been articulated by St. Thomas. Through the immediate labor of making, of writing poetry with a primary concern for the good of the thing made, they were discovering inescapable truths about art, inescapable because of the relation between made secondary worlds and the primary world created by God. Art by sophistry, art by an imposition of form through willed fancy, would truly make the made thing at best an imitation of an imitation, Plato's early quarrel with poetry in *The Republic*.

But the Fugitives' objection is not Plato's as we see it in *The*

Republic. Plato, holding creation to be a shadow of reality, therefore holds that art, insofar as it imitates that shadow, can itself be only shadow twice removed from the Ideal.[2] To the contrary, Davidson's objection is that, through devices of rhetoric that manipulate grammar and logic in order to ignore poetry's anchor in creation, the consequent poem is a work of fancy rather than of imagination. As a work of fancy, it exists primarily to serve the disturbed whim of the poet at the moment of its making.[3] That sort of poetry can only be, as Davidson's friend Robert Frost says approvingly, a "momentary stay against confusion." Frost, of course, is speaking of poetry at its best, in relation to himself as maker of poetry, and so there is finally a considerable distance between Frost's view on the matter and Davidson's. For poetry cannot be for Davidson, as it is for Frost, a game played by mind against creation. Though playful in his arguments and often in his poetry, Frost, too, is one of those homegrown Existentialists we spoke of earlier, much closer in his metaphysical understanding of man in nature to Wallace Stevens than to Davidson or Tate or Ransom, though I think one might be able to make an argument for kinships between Frost and Robert Penn Warren in this respect. (If one did so, however, I think one would conclude the voice in Frost's poetry more content with its game than Warren's.)

What I am suggesting is that the Fugitives had taken Coleridge to heart on the relation of fancy to imagination, but they do so from within what we might call a fundamentalist context to which they had been committed even before they began to think of themselves as poets, that "Southernness" of shared assumptions about society, man, nature, and God. For them, it became increasingly a concern that the faculty of the imagination, through its activity, should come to some root accommodation of form to reality through the created world. And they would do so without supposing that the created world is either the principal antagonist to mind as in Frost or a reservoir of matter for metaphor as with Stevens. Here indeed is the crux which becomes pivotal as the Fugitives turn to their Agrarian concerns. We shall find them objecting to the same sort of fanciful sophistry when it manipulates reality in the interest of an "industrial" mode as that sophistry

Davidson objects to in much of the poetry he encountered in the 1920s. In his "Mirror for Artists," his contribution to *I'll Take My Stand,* Davidson urges the artist to an active participation in community, the artist's having withdrawn from community in his "romantic" stage. "He must be a person first of all, even though for the time being he may become less of an artist. He must enter the common arena and become a citizen."

In the prefatory remarks to *I'll Take My Stand,* we find the point made that community is not to be restored by an education system "pouring in soft materials from the top," forcing a social form divorced of the limiting forms of human nature and of the natural world. Such would be form as dream, existing independently of reality, however real its advocates supposed it. The consequence of that manipulation is an arbitrary appropriation of the world's body and society's members to suit the dream. By such arbitrariness, existential reality, which should command our piety, can at once be denigrated and used perversely. The "Statement of Principles" insists that one is not to conclude that "proper living"—which is "a matter of intelligence and the will"—depends "on local climate or geography." Rather, it is "capable of a definition which is general and not Southern at all." That is, "proper living" is not determined by a provincial spirit which would limit its namings to "local climate or geography," as if the local so taken were of the essence.

Proper living is a universal potential, intrinsic in the particularities of creation, in the "logical pattern" of the world as separate from the logical pattern in the mind. For that distortion of "proper living" which makes it merely characteristic of local climate or geography is itself a nominalist action and as such a perversion of regional man. Chauvinistic Southerners, in other words, are as capable of distorting themselves into provincialists by a dependence upon local color as a justification of their being as any intellectual Manichaean who rejects all local climate and geography. We have only to observe the artificial coupling of local color to the industrial spirit, as for instance in the varieties of tourist attractions that abound, to recognize what can happen when local history submits to being packaged and sold to placeless wanderers.[4]

To our general argument we recall the title of one of John Crowe

Ransom's more famous essays on poetry, "The Concrete Universal." If in the Fugitives' early days Immanuel Kant is a considerable presence in their thought (and Kant will continue to be so for Ransom long after), the Kantean influence is another indication of their attempt to work back in Western thought to the point of thought's disjunction from feeling. Kant has kindly things to say of feeling in contrast to positions taken by Hume, Hobbes, or Locke, against whom the Fugitives also set their faces. For as thought had become separated from feeling, both had consequently been disjoined from reality, from the ground of both thought and feeling which lies in creation itself. The advocate of feeling, when he ignores reality, is no less culpable than the advocate of thought who does so. Davidson will warn particularly against this "Romantic" distortion of our full address to reality in his "Mirror for Artists": he says explicitly that the poet so inclined "exaggerates feeling at the expense of thought."

The few quotations above from *I'll Take My Stand,* along with our exploration of their meaning, ought to correct those who take their understanding of the Agrarian position from the likes of that *Macon Telegraph* editorial which Davidson quotes or from the writings of Ralph McGill, or from some more responsible academic critics who persist in misunderstanding the argument. Art, the Agrarians' preface says, "depends . . . like religion on a right attitude to nature." But those ceremonies of innocence, thought long since to have been drowned out of community, leaving in suspension the newly discovered "social sciences," were not quite drowned nor the waters quite dead. Already there is a beginning motion toward recovery when one can say in a troubled voice,

> What is this conversation, now secular,
> A speech not mine yet speaking for me in
> The heaving jelly of my tribal air?

Thus one begins to raise one's head above water and make swimming motions. The ceremony, the form, requires the myth.

But how was one to discover, in the 1920s in an academy in Tennessee, the ordinate relation of myth and form? It required of the poet, lyric or prophetic, a prosody carefully understood in the context of man's limited faculties. Those limited faculties must eventually engage large questions, especially metaphysical ones, given a disoriented age. One might reasonably conclude from the cultural history of the South that metaphysical questions had long been neglected, a failure in the community regrettable but understandable as one of the possible consequences of virtues long held in a community. That is, too easy an assumption of a common ground by community in its regard for society, man, nature, and God, if not articulated by the reason in its support of understanding, becomes distorted or lost. The "heaving jelly" of our "tribal air" was beginning to loose the aberrant spores feeding in it; but they carried few of the hopeful virtues of penicillin, except insofar as pollutions of mind and spirit prompted resistance to the contamination. The exception is that a discomfort in the body of community called some prophetic poets back to their responsibilities. The Southern Renaissance of letters occurred.

The most direct way to recovery, to a restoration of viable form in relation to myth, Davidson suggests, is to restore rhetoric to its proper respect and authority, toward ordering individual mind and consequently community. He quotes Tate's definition of rhetoric, given in an essay, "Is Literary Criticism Possible?" (1950):

> By rhetoric I mean the study and the use of figurative language of experience as the disciplines by which men govern their relations with one another in the light of truth. Rhetoric presupposes the study of two prior disciplines, grammar and logic.

This is to say that the mind—by reflection and practice, by study and use—comes into possession of its faculties and thereby into a possession of that most valuable of all communal properties, language. A common language is the significant enfranchisement in any community which is to maintain its vitality, its concert of individual minds each understanding and disciplining itself through language to the extent of its peculiar gifts. Indeed, such self-realization is the best gift an individual can make to community.

That had been the understanding, in the Ciceronian world, of what it meant to be members one of another within the body social, to which understanding was to be added St. Paul's figurative enlargement when he says to the New Romans (Romans 12:4ff.): "For as we have many members in one body, and all have not the same office: So we, being many, are one body in Christ, and every one members one of another." For we have "gifts differing according to the grace that is give to us," gifts whose limits we discover in community by the diligence of our "making" in relation to the general body of which we are member. We are committed to the "figurative language of experience" by our humanity. That is, we are committed to the discovery of analogy between our special gifts and the structure of creation, which is why man's general calling in nature is as steward of being, not creator of being. Thus the several actions of our making—each according to his particular gifts—are included in vital community, even that "figurative language" of the gardener or farmer or bricklayer or cook, no less than the seemingly more literal language of lawyers, judges, poets, and lecturers. For it is the language of our makings, in its several figurative reachings, that orients community "in the light of truth."

IT IS NOT EASY to recover known but forgotten things when they have been subjected to distortions in an effort to obliterate them. As we begin this recovery in respect to things Southern, however, we may begin to better appreciate the recent literal history of a place called the South, in which Cicero and English common law were decisive to community but decisive only as modified by that religious dimension of politics which enters and works its way westward from Constantine, settling almost as a sediment of history, in the eyes of its antagonists, in the "religious" South. One of those men born Yankees of that race of men, H. L. Mencken, gained points with the popular mind by ridiculing the South as a "Bible Belt." What Mencken and others like-minded with him accomplished by such attacks was not a purifying but a stirring up of the waters in the Southern swamp, so that the spiritual became increasingly a public, a political question. Indeed, we may be more indebted to Mencken for the reactivation of Fundamentalism than he would wish to think. At that turning moment, in the 1920s, such a consequence hardly seemed likely. In response to Mencken and others, a confused alarm was raised in the South, a defensiveness not well articulated as a rule. The response seemed very much to suit its antagonists in the courts of public opinion. The "backward" South was a last bastion of antiquated religion, the solution to which was sociological analysis, to be followed by the institution of programs of education poured in from the top; that is, from Washington. Old-time religion and hookworm were almost made cause and effect. With Southern minds in confusion, it was not difficult to score points in the national popular mind at the South's expense, points whose afterimage is with us still in the portrayal of stereotyped Southerners on national television "dramas." Just how valuable the South has been to the progressive mind in its direction of public affairs is difficult to measure, but the South as laughingstock and whipping boy certainly allowed that mind to shift attention away from serious questions. Indeed, how welcome to that mind seemed the Scopes Trial at Dayton, Tennessee, in 1925.

Two Southerners in particular, Donald Davidson and John Crowe Ransom, became aware of what was at issue in that famous trial as they watched the effects from close at hand. Their Chancellor's response was that more laboratories were called for at Vanderbilt University. Ransom's was the publication of *God Without Thunder: An Unorthodox Defense of Orthodoxy* (1930). But not many beyond the young Fugitives were prepared to see that the trial, as Davidson says, was not "a contest between religious bigotry and enlightened science. . . . the cardinal issue was the right of the state, through its legislature, to control and administer instruction in its public schools." The recognition on Davidson's part led him to begin writing a "kind of poetry I had not practiced in the closed circle of the Fugitive group." So popular has that famous trial become in the public mind, so much a matter of folklore infused and kept alive by the media, that many of the salient circumstances are long since lost to the popular mind, though they were decisive in leading the Twelve Southerners to a position in *I'll Take My Stand.*

The hard core of the matter at issue, rather surely, is the one Davidson points to, and the increasing loss of control of the states' educational systems to centralized government may be marked from this trial, although the conclusive effect was federal money to state education after World War II: that seals the fate of the state's right in regard to its educational institutions.[5] It is difficult to make clear briefly the importance of Richard Weaver's analysis of the trial itself, his point that the argument of Darrow and the defense was that evolution is true, while the argument of the prosecutor Bryan was that its teaching was unlawful. The roles of the parties to the dispute have been largely reversed in the interim, in respect to prayer in schools, for instance. For increasingly the higher courts have difficulty in defending the position that public prayer is unlawful in the face of the swelling tide of conviction in the public mind that public prayer is salutary to public virtue and is therefore a "true" necessity in public education. As Mencken is in part a source of that swelling tide, through his epithets out of the trial ("Bible Belt," "Monkey Trial," the local citizenry described as "gaping primates" or "anthropoid rabble"), Darrow may well prove in the end a cause of amended laws or a constitutional article restoring the right to prayer in schools; his wily distortion of the rules of law and order opened doors unnoticed in 1925.

Among the historical elements of the popular myth of the Scopes Trial as it comes to us are certain facts embarrassing to recall and therefore seldom mentioned. That is, embarrassing to recall by that manipulative mind for whom this particular myth is to be used to impose order poured in from the top upon a recalcitrant "Southern" mind. For instance, a New Yorker (George Rappleyea) and a Dayton druggist (F. E. Robinson) persuaded young Scopes to be arrested and indicted by the county grand jury. The idea sprang from an ad in the *Chattanooga Times* run by the American Civil Liberties Union which promised to support anyone challenging the Tennessee law that forbade the teaching of evolution as established truth. The New Yorker was local manager of a defunct mine; the druggist a native interested in local prosperity. Such a trial might put Dayton on the map, attract industry and investment. (The druggist sold "Monkey Fizzes" to the crowds gathered for the show, this being long before the day of the Possum Frisbee.) Scopes himself, a temporary substitute for an ailing biology teacher, was to say later, "To tell the truth, I wasn't sure I had taught evolution." The trial, then, was hardly one concerned with principle; it was rather a managed happening in the interest of individual reputations (Mencken's, Darrow's, Bryan's) and local prosperity.[6] In the the popular myth, however, truth and high principle are understood as end and cause.

Such a spectacle as the Scopes Trial was possible, I am suggesting, because "Southerners" had not sufficiently addressed those large questions, particularly the metaphysical ones. They had become complacently dependent upon the letter of the law, neglecting the metaphysical dimensions which alone can make law more than arbitrary form. If we insist on the doctrine of the separation of Church and State, it does not follow that there is no reciprocal relation between the two, though having lost an understanding of reciprocity we fall into confusions on either hand; it is an error in the Fundamentalist position to suppose its rescue to lie in the letter of the law. It is a deliberate blindness of destructive effect for civil libertarians to deny any relevance of metaphysics to the letter of the law.

The young Fugitives could no longer put off those large questions; neither can we. As there are reciprocal "faculties" in the body of community, there have been separations of the individual soul's faculties of the *ratio* and *intellectus,* of the head and heart; we may not deny at the highest reach of our thought—understanding—their desirable concert. It seems desirable that a person's several faculties, while distinct within the person's soul, cannot be at war with each other but must hold easy commerce if the person is to be whole. As of the individual, so too of family or a community of individuals. By the figurative language of experience—by analogy—we conclude that this principle (the soul's faculties in concert within the individual) may be operative in family and community taken as bodies; the several membership of those discrete bodies of community and family must establish easy commerce also.

Such a belief follows from the belief that we, as peculiar individuals—that is, as discretely differing creatures of Providence—are nevertheless members of a general existence, members of the large body of creation. The poet awakening to these realizations knows that his language becomes crucial not only to his individual integrity but to the integrity of the family and community to which he finds himself committed by his discoveries. Words can no longer be simply in the service of private whim or private distress, though it does not follow of course that either family or community dictate the poet's service. It rather means that the poet is the more deeply committed in his own responsibilities to words in relation to the truth of reality, to a concern for the good of the thing he makes. He knows then that, insofar as he so addresses himself, his makings are consequential to community health. His position in community is not official, as is that of judge or governor. But it is crucial, as is the similar relationship of the ninth part of speech to the academy's eight and as is metaphysics to law.

Allen Tate, in the definition of rhetoric we have quoted, asserts rhetoric to be the study of "figurative language." Rather certainly, he does not intend that phrase to mean that language is a decoration imposed by mind, though figurative language, often spoken of as "poetic" language, has come to mean for us a use of language which is not serious about reality, about the way "it really is." Sentimentality, we have seen, is in part responsible for the difficulty any poet has in being taken seriously by community, though poets, too, have been repeatedly at fault for their disenfranchisement. We see the saloon dandy's verbal plumage gracing cocktail chatter, as with Eliot's Prufrock or Pound's Lady Valentine. But the ironic and sardonic tones in these poets' portraits show the poets themselves rejecting as inadequate even so learned and witty a mind as Prufrock's or even so culturally certified a person as Lady Valentine. On the other hand, I do not believe Tate intends to address primarily that sort of figurative language we have characterized as necessary to, though ultimately inadequate to, the visionary experience. We have already recalled the poet of "Ash-Wednesday" attempting to deal with mystical experience, attempting to bear witness to an experience of personhood touched by grace. While such experience, cast in figurative language, is a vital influence on community, it rather feeds community secretly through its members at a level of the private rather than the public. It does not follow that such experience of the ineffable is not to be spoken of in public, only that the prophetic poet is more directly vatic than mystic. Mystical vision is delicately private, though not obscene. I have in mind here such mystical witness as that borne by the anonymous poet of *The Cloud of Unknowing,* or St. John of the Cross's *Dark Night of the Soul* or *Ascent of Mount Carmel,* or Dame Julian of Norwich's *Revelations of Divine Love.* These are works valued by a Tate or an Eliot, but not because their use of figurative language is so immediate to the disciplines by which men govern their relations with each other, though they feed those disciplines through their feeding of the souls of the prophetic poet. One contrasts such "poems," for instance, to poems like the *Aeneid* or *Divine Comedy* or *Paradise Lost* or *The Waste Land* in attempting a delicate distinction.

Davidson, in quoting Tate on the study of figurative language as a public concern, asks whether the writer needs a formal education. The question applies more largely than to the writer, and his answer is, of course, positive. The decline in such attention to formal education left Davidson, for instance, to conclude it "horrifying to see the cause of liberal education argued in a Tennessee court by a famous agnostic lawyer" when liberal education was not actually the immediate concern at issue. As for the poet himself, both Tate and Davidson know that it is part of his responsibility "To purify the dialect of the tribe / And urge the mind to aftersight and foresight"—that is, by an attention to language to clarify mind's action in and toward a concern for community, if community is not to disintegrate. (I borrow the quotation from Eliot's *Little Gidding,* a poem which shares Tate's argument against the decay of that most valuable community property, language.)

Tate is opposing a decay of language through which it is reduced to the literal, as is the tendency of language in an unreflective, pragmatic age—an age dominantly given to commerce in things through abstractions of creation. That is the most destructive effect of the "industrial" mind which the Agrarians opposed in their manifesto. As the Agrarians recognized also, language suffers when "science" narrows from its larger inclusiveness, so that its language strives toward a one-to-one correspondence of sign to signified. Both conditions have contributed to the disintegration of language, in consequence of which one prophetic poet cried out to us,

> Things fall apart; the center cannot hold;
> Mere anarchy is loosed upon the world,
> The blood-dimmed tide is loosed, and everywhere
> The ceremony of innocence is drowned;
> The best lack all conviction, while the worst
> Are full of passionate intensity.

Yeats's words, spoken in 1921, fit rather well those local circumstances of a Southern scene in Tennessee in 1925, making us see the Scopes Trial a more universal event than it seemed. Davidson recognized it so, his "Fire on Belmont Street" the immediate response.

In a decaying community such as we have characterized, though it is not necessarily localized, one begins to see being through assigned values. Put another way: one begins to see creation as an effect of applied formulae as in inorganic chemistry, a reductionism at work in complex creation at the level where literal symbol is taken as vision. One sees Nominalism pragmatically applied to creation. Thus when we see the Scopes "Monkey" Trial as a sort of modern Morality Play, Chancellor Kirkland's response is understandable. What is needed in such trying times for one who is born Yankee of the race of men is for the universities to build more laboratories. His is the reaction of mind toward an embrace of ideology, toward idol worship, in which the literal symbol becomes the idol, keeping the moiling complexities of creation somewhat at bay. It is the act of a mind which, having lost its figurative language, is busy making "what will suffice." An alternate response of a similar mind might be the proliferation of metaphor in which language is divorced of the realities which raise the metaphysical questions. That is the direction in which Wallace Stevens responds to the confusions of mind in the 1920s, as my phrase from "Of Modern Poetry" shows.

If the Agrarians are right, a figurative language of experience is crucial to men in community if they are to govern their relations with one another in the full light of truth. There is a truth, certainly, expressed in such a name as H_2O, but it is a truth which has not yet begun to approach city drinking water and sewage systems, to speak nothing of the healing properties associated with water in those ceremonies of innocence from prehistoric times down to our own, associations made through myth believed. Because of the complexity of creation, including the variety of minds struggling to accommodate variety and unity in a community, a literal language is inadequate since it understands symbolization only as the arbitrary act of mind providing what will suffice. Tate's concern in his definition of rhetoric turns out to be the one Davidson voices in his "Ninth Part of Speech," a concern that we regain through formal training that old, now largely abandoned ideal of liberal education. That ideal, as understood at Plato's Academy and in the medieval schools, is rather effectively summarized in Tate's definition of rhetoric with slight additions of my own: one acquires, through the study of and use of the figurative language of an experience, to be found in those monuments of unaging intellect inherited from our fathers, those necessary disciplines of head and heart by which men govern their relations with one another in the continuing community of humanity, under that community's commitment through good will to the full light of truth.

Such a statement brings together St. Paul, St. Thomas, Yeats, Weaver, Eric Voegelin, Eliot, Davidson, Tate, and a host of others past and present in a resistance to the corrosive presence of gnosticism in community. That Tate certainly has in mind such concert is everywhere apparent in his work. That he means in this limited sample we have used an endorsement of its efficacy as a principle of public education is apparent from his carefully acknowledged certification of the traditional structure of the liberal education, derived from classical and scholastic models.[7]

MR. DAVIDSON, in the second of his Lamar Lectures, summarizes the intentions of the Agrarian in *I'll Take My Stand.* "We were saying that life should determine economics, and not economics life. Our quarrel was not with industry or science in their proper roles, but with industrialism as a tryant enslaving and ruling science itself, and with it religion, the arts, education, the state, thus reducing all principles to one principle, the economic, and becoming a destroyer, ready to break the continuity of human history and threatening the very existence of human society." One should remember that the Agrarian position was sharply opposed to both communism and the brand of capitalism whose metaphysical position, as Solzhenitsyn was to point out in his shocking Commencement Address at Harvard in 1974, is essentially the same: a position which sees power as the only god. Solzhenitsyn's words, which proved widely disturbing not only to the left but to the comfortable right, draw the parallel:

> the mistake must be at the root, at the very basis of human thinking in the past centuries. It is the prevailing Western view of the world which was born during the Renaissance and found its political expression starting in . . . the Enlightenment. It became the basis for government and social sciences and could be defined as rationalistic humanism or humanistic autonomy: the proclaimed and enforced autonomy of man from any higher source above him.

It is hardly surprising that President Ford refused to receive this outland creature, nor that liberal intellectuals were offended by him. How similar, then, the Russian dissident's message to us and that of the Agrarians over forty years earlier. Given their rejection of modernist mind, wherever it be located, we understand why even now, in a period marked by a resurgence of what is popularly called "conservatism," there continues a suspicion of the Agrarians as of Solzhenitsyn from both sides of the political spectrum.[8]

In the spring of 1933, Donald Davidson was staying at Marshallville, a few miles from our lectern, as guest of one of the Twelve Southerners, John Donald Wade, who was to be head of the English Department and founding editor of the *Georgia Review* at the University of Georgia. Word came that Seward Collins, then editor of *The Bookman,* was interested in founding a periodical to be called the *American Review.* In Davidson's words, "he wished to found a new magazine . . . for the special purpose of publishing the writings of four groups of traditionalists or conservatives: the Humanists of the North, the Neo-Thomists of France and America, the Distributists of England, and the Agrarians of the South."[9] The meeting with the Agrarians was to be at Andrew Lytle's farm home in Guntersville, Alabama. Davidson traveled to it by bus, and on his return, after the stimulating conversations, found himself stranded, waiting for a bus for several hours in Rome, Georgia. He walked about the town and nearby countryside, the recent conversations no doubt heightening his observation. Twenty-five years later he recalls the hours vividly. There was the statue of Bedford Forrest. There was the bronze she-wolf suckling Romulus and Remus. From an elevation he could see the confluence of the Coosa and the Oostanaula form the Etowah, whose Indian names would not escape Davidson's sense of resonance in the names of things. It was also a sparkling Sabbath day in spring, and as he strolled through the community cemetery he came upon a Confederate monument with an anonymous inscription. The tribute is to those dead who came, not from the plantation slavery South but from the yeoman uplands, again a point of significance to us as to Donald Davidson. The inscription reads in part:

> This monument is the testimony of the present to the future that these were they who kept the faith as it was given them by the fathers. Be it known by this token that these men were true to the traditions of their lineage. . . . To their sons they left but honor and their country. Let this stone forever warn those who keep these valleys that only their sires are dead; the principles for which they fought can never die.

A rich confluence of places, events, principles haunts this episode in Davidson's life as we reflect on it. We have already introduced, for instance, the relevance of that Neo-Thomist Etienne Gilson and Jacques Maritain, whose *Art and Scholasticism* was to be important to Eric Gill and the Distributists, particularly to G. K. Chesterton, to say nothing of an influence on that great historian, Christopher Dawson. And *Art and Scholasticism* was to be valued by Allen Tate and Caroline Gordon and became central to Flannery O'Connor's aesthetics. Maritain would already have appeared in the *Criterion,* some of him translated by Eliot. Ford Madox Ford was to be drawn to the Agrarians and their concerns, as would be such interesting and diverse people as Robert Lowell and Randall Jarrell and, of course, Miss O'Connor. And in those years immediately following Davidson's Sunday epiphany in Rome, Georgia, he would write *The Attack on Leviathan.* Ransom would follow *God*

Without Thunder with his defense of *The World's Body* (1938) in which literature's balance of heart and head is pursued. Eliot's *After Strange Gods* (1933) would presently side with the Agrarian position against a common enemy, now rather more clearly seen by those young Vanderbilt poets, who were steadily in pursuit of metaphysical questions as those questions are anchored in nature and history.

The ferment of traditionalist thought in Europe and America was rather further advanced than the Fugitives could know in the 1920s, and an ally was emerging in Vienna whose considerable support of their position has yet to be adequately appreciated.[10] Having read voraciously in Western philosophy and history and literature, having learned Greek that he might come to terms with Plato, Eric Voegelin began that journey of history which stands now as one of the great monuments of unaging intellect, *Order and History.* The year Davidson's *Attack on Leviathan* was published, Voegelin was fired from his Austrian position as Extraordinary Professor at Vienna, Hitler having taken over his country. Fleeing Austria into Switzerland, he came at last to the University of Alabama as an assistant professor, then to Louisiana State University, where Cleanth Brooks and Robert Penn Warren were getting the *Southern Review* under way. There Voegelin began a lifelong friendship with Brooks.

That rich confluence, which we have focused in relation to the heroic epitaph in the Rome, Georgia, cemetery and Donald Davidson's encounter of it, brings us at last to Voegelin's telling identification and adumbration of the enemy Davidson speaks of, the creator as Davidson puts it of the "new barbarism . . . controlled and directed by the modern power state." Voegelin, the author of *The Authoritarian State* (1936), which precipitated his exile, would have recognized that common enemy at once.[11] Its agents he was to characterize as deconstructors of being, would-be directors of restructured existence, in seminal books of increasing influence in Western thought and of particular relevance to the "Southernness" we pursue: *The New Science of Politics* (1952); *Science, Politics, and Gnosticism* (1968); *From Enlightenment to Revolution* (1975); and his multivolume history of the Western mind, *Order and History.*

The enemy, says Voegelin, may be designated the new gnostic, whose one principle of operation in the world is to acquire and use power over being. From that principle it follows as a first necessity the deconstruction of reality, the separation of mind into an autonomy independent of reality. That is, the mind must separate itself from the complexity of being in order to manipulate being. If we may borrow St. Thomas's terms to the point, the particular *ens* must stand clear of *esse,* whereby it declares *esse* the prime matter with which a dream universe generated by that detached mind is to be constituted. In the words of a local academic leader who is enthusiastic about the prospects, mind through gnosis wills to "reprogram nature," making use of all the technology available, including presumably the technology of mind programming itself. Being is to be reinvented. The ends posited as ultimate realities are presumptuous acts out of the gnostic mind's pretense to godhead, in which respect the new gnostic differs from the ancient gnostic, who always posited the existence of God. We are encountering here, be it noted, the New Alchemist disguised in the worshipped robes of academic science. That such an attempt is doomed one believes on the evidence of the history of failures in our century, especially of totalitarian politics and war, though the immediate destructions from those attempts are hardly encouraging. That this same perverse force is harbored in the Western democracies the Agrarians, Voegelin, Solzhenitsyn, and others have warned us.

One believes the gnostic attempt upon the heart of being is doomed on the evidence increasingly available, but also on faith, faith being the consent in us beyond knowledge (gnosis)—a willingness of surrender at risk to that which is beyond the limits of both our being and our knowing. Ultimately that to which we surrender belief is beyond *ens* and *esse,* beyond the complex creation within which we must exercise not only knowledge but faith. Thus is "knowledge / carried to the heart," in Tate's phrase. Tate remarks, incidentally, that these lines in his "Ode to the Confederate Dead" refer "to Pascal's war between heart and head, between *finesse* and *geometrie.*" He understands that his poem, as he would understand that memorial inscription in the Rome cemetery, engages principles more deeply at issue in the War Between the States than our modern histories of that conflict at present acknowledge. And that is why Voegelin's work is so important to an appreciation of the Agrarian position.

One's faith that modern gnosticism is doomed does not mean, however, that doomed gnosis, given its desire for reprogramming nature, does not cause immediate and even general miseries to one's faith, let alone to one's substance. The history of Stalin and Hitler is quite immediate still, sufficiently so that one feels a moment of terror no less than anger when that academic leader I mentioned asserts as the academy's goal the "reprogramming of nature." If the words mean anything at all, they imply a belief in nature as merely mechanical, nature's own programming a matter of cosmic accident now superseded by autonomous man. For nowhere in the wash of this academic leader's verbiage is there acknowledgment either of a "Programmer" above man or of that question's being still an open one in responsible minds. What such words actually record is a portion of doomed history, since existence is more complex and unyielding to gnosis than acknowledged or recognized by such would-be time lords. If the Renaissance alchemists dreamed of a homunculus, ours are confident of having made theirs, the computer.[12] But except by fundamental destruction, existence is not to be reduced out of time to the control of gnosis incarnate, the computer.

Voegelin describes the conditions of existence which make it but an illusion to suppose that one may stand aside from nature to manipulate it. It is an illusion because in the very act of standing aside, one carries with him that very complexity he attempts to avoid, his own complex being. The focal point of reality is always the individual soul as it responds to the complexity of creation. Here, then, is Voegelin's description of the existence of consciousness in reality, inextricables:

> Existence has the structure of the In-Between, of the Platonic metaxy, and if anything is constant in the history of mankind it is the language of tension between life and death, immortality and mortality, perfection and imperfection, time and timelessness, between order and disorder, truth and untruth, sense and senselessness of existence; between *amor Dei* and *amor sui*, *l'ame ouverte* and *l'ame close;*

> between the virtues of openness toward the ground of being such as faith, hope and love and the vices of infolding closure such as hybris and revolt; between the moods of joy and despair; and between alienation in its double meaning of alienation from the world and alienation from God. If we split these pairs of symbols, and hypostatize the poles of tension as independent entities, we destroy the reality of existence . . . ; we lose consciousness and intellect; we deform our humanity and reduce ourselves to a state of quiet despair or activist conformity to the "age." . . . In the language of Heraclitus and Plato: Dream life usurps the place of wake life.

When we split the poles, we do so only by having separated within ourselves those faculties of the soul given us so that we may find our place in the confines of time. This is the destructive separation we have been arguing all along, the "dissociation of sensibilities," the separation of thought and feeling, head and heart, the destructive breach between the *ratio* and the *intellectus*.

If we wonder why Johnny can't read or write or sing—Johnny here meaning most of us, whether Freshman or College President, Business Executive or Sunday School Teacher—we must not look only to the failed mechanics of instruction as the explanation, if by such mechanics we mean formulae poured in from the top by gnostic presumption. That was an explicit warning in the opening pages of *I'll Take My Stand* which was ignored. As much as I am encouraged by the current concern that we get back to the basics in our education, I cannot believe such a return alone will be worth the while if we do not recognize that we must get all the way back to the most basic, back to the ground of being, out of which only may grow habits of thought, and words appropriate to thought, that will make thought worthwhile. The mechanics of grammar or math or science are summoned out of the realities of nature and human nature. If severed from their origins in the ninth part of speech, if words are divorced from anchor in the structure of existence, removed from the In-Between, they become so many gleeks, bloops, and gonks to be fed into the machine of the ear with preconceived expectations of response. That is inevitable, to the degree by which we ignore the "ninth part of speech." Those expectations are out of a very primitive level of intellect, approximating in its faith the alchemist's faith that he can transmute elements, however modern and advanced they are argued to be.

When language is accepted by the popular spirit as merely neural stimuli in the biology of the cortex of animal man, the unfortunate consequence is very likely to be the anticipated neural response. Word-shocked sheep look up and think they're fed. And that is precisely what is intended by the gnostic directors of being. If we do not see the student as a creature gifted by intellect, pushing against the borders of his own ignorance and ours; if we do not see ourselves as just such students, then neither money nor the "basics" we try to buy with money will save us from confusion. That is an old lesson one might have learned from Socrates, except that there is little room in any curriculum at any university for us to encounter Socrates except by accident. The gnostic director is in charge of our minds, declaring that the university's role is to develop a "capacity to forge progress," devoted to the "search for new knowledge and information," both of which are accorded equal dignity in this statement of purpose (quoted from a university president, let me assure you).[13] Nor are we properly persuaded by the multiplication of machinery *per se* in our institutions of learning. What boots it that each professor of philosophy has a word processor, if that advantage serves only to make idiocy prolific? How, indeed, does the addition of laboratories address the Morality Play about modernity, the Scopes Trial?

If Johnny cannot read, he senses the deprivation at least. And he has a sufficient residual common sense to know the cause somehow built into the system. Feeling himself possessed by vague abstractionism that separates him from an engagement with the In-Between, little wonder he rebels. Disinherited, the young focus the frenzy of a residual, emaciated piety on some hapless particular, usually a specter that is but symptom of the loss of being. Why should we be surprised by marches and riots directed against hot-dog stands that skimp on mustard or onions when the object of spiritual hunger in our restless selves has been distorted by the elevation of the abstract to the status of absolute reality? That such a lost estate is our immediate problem I think I can illustrate with a brief catalog of events and quotations, random and disparate, though with a common ground to their freakisheness. For these are all actions and words speaking the loss of old anchor in reality.

From Hollywood: As an instance of what Voegelin speaks of as a "state of quiet despair," Marilyn Monroe's statement that she believed in everything—a little.

Another from Hollywood: Judy Belushi, in that popular journal of the public spirit *People* (June 1984, p. 116), remembering her husband, John, dead of a drug overdose: "Lorne [Michaels, the original producer of *Saturday Night Live*] said something that I found very moving: 'He [John Belushi] died for our sins.' I hope people can understand that." (If people only could, *People* would very quickly go bankrupt.)

From the news media: June 21, 1983, an ABC evening news report on children's abuse of their parents: The expert consulted finds no discernible ethnic or economic denominator in the cases examined; he does find that children of the 1970s are three times as likely to commit violence against parents and siblings as children of the 1950s. One researcher reports a parent's pleading, "What can I do?" Which means, says the researcher, that the children are in charge of the family. In a circular argument, the expert points to the dissolution of the family as the principal factor involved.

September 16, 1982, a CBS interview with one whose title is "Negotiations Expert": This expert explains how he handled a particular squabble among his own children over the last piece of pie at supper: "I explained that we could all go to Mommie and get her to make another pie."

January 1985, Reuters News Agency: "Pierre Beaumard, a Frenchman suffering from an inability to relate to other people and from various obsessional fears, attended a therapy group where the psychotherapist encouraged Beaumard to sandwich himself between two mattresses while other members walked over him to 'stamp out his complexes.' After several minutes of this treatment, Beaumard was crushed to death."

September 22, 1984, a reporter on Atlanta's WSB, with a new entry for the next Guinness book of world records: "Mr. ____ is believed to be the first man convicted of raping his comatose wife in Georgia."

And, from closer to home, the beginning of football season, a directive from a group called "Spirit Galore in '74!"—which almost makes one nostalgic for the French Directorate: "This year the Spirit Committee at ____ is making every effort to cover our stadium with Red & Black. Please try to make your football clothes our colors so that our boys can not only hear your spirit—but see your spirit!"

And finally, some inspiring words from the leader of academic mind already cited: "Beneath all the sound and fury of our day-to-day operations, there exists a unifying thread that pervades this University. . . . That thread, that bond, is a universal commitment to the highest ideals of education."

Little wonder one is inclined to shout, "Flee to the hills. The life you save may be your own."

WE HAVE BEEN CONCERNED to notice, in the course of our argument, a dissolution of community through its loss of a vision of reality, the chief burden of our modernism. I have not meant by community simply a small, homogeneous gathering of people in the limited geography of place. I would be among the last to abandon such an incarnation of community in a local, limited gathering, as well as the last to insist that those temporal limits are absolute requirement. If such a community exists, or ever has since the breakup of the first family and the murder of Abel by Cain, it must of necessity concentrate the vices of fallen man no less than his virtues, so that such a community made into an idol by fancy's ignoring the vices would be no more acceptable a correspondence to complex reality than would any Utopian community projected a millennium ahead of us. What I rather mean by community we recognize in those more comfortable moments of our journey through the world when we feel that we belong. We recognize this sense in companionship, as various as that within family or with old or even random friends. We recognize it in moments of openness shared with an old man or woman or a child or persons anywhere in between. And when we are caught up in such companionable moments, we discover that the particularities of place are amenable in a particular way; very often we may discover that the particular place does indeed feed the estate of community. I find myself more comfortably aware of a community, in my own circumstance, in Crawford, in Oglethorpe County. But I am confident that Solzhenitsyn, in his little novel *One Day in the Life of Ivan Denisovich,* has made persuasive argument for the existence of community in so inhospitable and detached a place as the Soviet concentration camps in Siberia.

What is important in community is the shared recognition of the value of existence, through which recognition one distinguishes. Some things and actions are to be chosen and held, others rejected. Some ways of choosing and acting are to be valued, others condemned as violations of being beyond those violations that are always necessary consequences of existence itself. For by being we do violence in a sense; to breathe we violate the air. The salad we eat instead of flesh may cry out to the sensitive ear; we must learn the importance of that piety of deportment toward being that ameliorates the inescapable violence of our becoming. In doing so, we begin to learn the limits of violence. In the light of such realities about existence, let us say that there is a recognizable commonality in "humanity": that which we may, with care and attention, call the basis of civilized community. If we can speak so, we know already what Donald Davidson means when he says that the young Fugitives began to feel "the cause of civilized society" under attack by distorted forces of the mind, increasingly evident as "the new barbarism of science and technology controlled and directed by the modern power state."

In this regard, it is very worth our remembering what Paul Johnson, in *Modern Times,* describes as "the institutionalization of modernism" in the Weimar Republic. The battle became increasingly engaged between the invading Western *Zivilisation* and

German *Kultur.* The invader, degenerate and decadent, from the German point of view, threatened the native. A generation of German scholars took pains to separate the two, establishing the primacy of *Kultur* in the *Volk,* over the perversity of *Zivilisation.* The very localizing of the desirable culture in the folk of a particular tribal heritage provided an impetus Hitler seized upon. What we might conclude, and it is one of the ironies of history, is that this first engagement of the West with Hitler was in the realm of idea in which a specialized abstraction of a tribal people from the complex of reality allowed Hitler to command a sufficient collective power to undertake a general reprogramming of the whole world. Hitler's is an abstractionism camouflaged so skillfully by the local as to appear anchored in reality to the naive mind. To accomplish his end, he had to reject certain of those "Southern" principles we have argued to be universal and not local. We declare with Stark Young that we defend principles in creation, universal principles, not because they belong to the South, but because the South belongs to them. It was Hitler's position that the principles worth holding belonged to the German people; in this respect, though there are conspicuous correspondences between Nazi and Soviet totalitarianism, the Nazi program differs from the Soviet. For it is the Soviet position that the universals exist independent of all concrete particulars, a sort of perverse Platonism whereby the manipulation of particulars is justified. Hitler says of his gnostic program: from here we move outward. Lenin and Stalin say of theirs: from this abstract detachment, we move in and everywhere at once.

In our own argument we have suggested that "Southernness" is first of all a state of soul, not a condition in nature, and we have pointed to the individual soul as the locus of a disjunction of vision which prevents the ordinate love of place in community, and consequently to the mutual support of each community and nature. That locus is not so much in time and place, nor in programs generalized nor constitutions subscribed; in the particulars of programs one discovers effects of success or failure, as opposed to causes of success or failure of community, though in those same particulars are clearly imprinted the cause. For that reason our words and actions in nature are means whereby we journey to recognition of their cause in the individual soul. The cause of our loss of vision is dis-fusion, in contrast to the con-fusion, vision, within individual souls, for vision is a matter of the particular soul's fullness in seeing. I have argued the dis-fusion a separation of the soul's faculties, the heart's and head's separation by willfulness. The separation occurs through the will's intent to gnostic power, power first over the being of the particular soul and then by extension over being in general. That illusion is possible to maintain only so long as one faculty is dominant. The faculty that has come to dominate our age, we have insisted, is the *ratio,* but we should be endangered if, seeing that power pervasive of the popular mind, we should then react by an inordinate embrace of the sister power, the understanding of the heart. That has been, too often, the response of the artist since the eighteenth century, leaving mind embattled with itself first and then with the world.

Allen Tate, in his contribution to *I'll Take My Stand* ("Remarks on Southern Religion"), talks of this division, though not in the terms we have used. He argues metaphorically, talking about the horse, where we have been more general in talking of reality. The horse, he says, is a creature modern man manipulates, not seeing its native wholeness. "The modern mind sees only half of the horse—that half which may become a dynamo, or an automobile, or any other horsepowered machine." Thus modern man overvalues half a horse, but with religious fervor. "A religion of the half-horse is preeminently a religion of how things work. . . . We know that the cult [out of this knowledge] of infallible working is a religion because it sets up an irrational value; it is irrational to believe in omnipotent human rationality." Yet this is the "American religion," against which Tate sets a Southern resistance, which he nevertheless suspects doomed to failure.

As for those Southerners who resist, "they were capable of using their horses, as they did one day at Brandy Station, but they could also contemplate them as absolute and inviolable objects; they were virtually incapable of abstracting from the horse his horsepower, or from history its historicity," gnostic actions necessary to the manipulation of nature in which Tate finds the New England mind adept. I am dwelling on Tate's essay here for several reasons, not the least of which is to indicate how large a view Tate holds of community and how deeply he, and Davidson, understood that the roots of vision lie in the complexity of reality. What Tate laments is a Southern failure to have established its vision. Very early, he says, the South began its abandonment in favor of the half-horse. There is a dangerous division in the Western mind, he suggests, in contrast to the Eastern Orthodox mind "whose religion is quite simply supernaturalism of the naive religion of the whole horse. It never suspects the existence of those halves that render our sanity so precarious and compel us to vacillate between a self-destroying naturalism and practicality, on the one hand, and a self-destroying mysticism, on the other. . . . we cannot let the entire horse fill our minds all at once, as it does the Eastern mind." We cannot, because we cannot contemplate the religious qualities of the horse without first setting aside its "merely spatial and practicable half," which is equivalent to holding only the *other* half of the horse. If Tate used Flannery O'Connor's terms, he would say that the dangerous division in the Western mind is its constant bent toward Manichaeanism.

And thus, he continues, we in the West have a special notion of tradition—"a notion that tradition is not simply a fact, but a fact that must be constantly defended." From this preparation, Tate pays tribute to the older Western church's solution to this Western dilemma of the separation of the *intellectus* and *ratio,* with its always threatening dissociation of the soul's sensibilities. The scholastics, "by making Reason, Science, or Nature, an instrument of defense for the protection of the other than reasonable," specifically defended myth and symbol, thereby performing the "only kind of unity that the Western mind is capable of." It was a unity destroyed by the men of the Renaissance, who said: "Throw over the spirits and symbols, which are irrational anyhow, not rationally necessary, and find those quantities in nature which will *work.*" Through myth and symbol, nature had been maintained as inviolable, but once the rational mind proved them fiction rather than fact, "nature became simply a workable half," the half-horse to be used in secular man's journey to Utopia.

In 1930, then, Tate is talking about movements in the Western mind that Richard Weaver, Eric Voegelin, Mircea Eliade, Alexander Solzhenitsyn, and others will be talking about in the post–World War II years. The difference is that in those later years there will be an audience more willing to listen, since the effects of the religion of the half-horse are more conspicuous. This said, we return to our point: it is unquestionable, I believe, that the dissociation of head and heart has accelerated in the Western mind since Nominalism's triumph over St. Thomas; and we may and must explore the emerging gnostic force in its historical context. But insofar as we are concerned individually to know and understand the consequences of the new idol, as we go about reclaiming our "Southernness," we must be very clear that it is first and most important to know ours to be an individual action within our particular soul. That is the first possum to catch. And in respect to the history of modern gnosticism, we will discover at any point along the way that, while heart appears dominant in the popular spirit at one time and head at another, an individual soul at any time is not necessarily consumed by the dominant spirit of its age. There were "romantics"—in that popular naming of the heart's ascendancy—in the Age of Reason, as there were rationalists in the Romantic Age. If we, as a community, must deal most directly with the dominant distortion in our own day, we are better prepared by the light of its history; but we must realize that to deal effectively with it requires first our individual wholeness, which we must constantly strive for, though seldom perfect. If we throw out the present age's half-horse merely in favor of the other half, we will have still missed the whole horse. This, I suspect, is the basic weakness in the rising popular ecological concern, a valid direction but one unanchored in metaphysics and hence largely bent on substituting the other half of the horse.

"How," asks Mr. Tate at the end of his essay, "may a Southerner take hold of his tradition?" That is, how may one reclaim that whole horse which has been pulled apart since the Renaissance? His answer, directed to the citizenry of the South in the 1930s, is at first a shocking one. It must be "by violence," since the Southerner he addresses "cannot fall back upon his religion, simply because it was never articulated and organized for him." Let me hasten to add that Mr. Tate does not mean a violence such as had so recently turned Russia into a general slaughtering ground of millions, the slaughter enlarging under Stalin even as Tate's essay was published.[14] He means a political activism such as has indeed arisen in the South and spread outward since 1930, an activism we have spoken of in one of its manifestations as the appearance of Fundamentalism in the public arena. The Southerner, Mr. Tate says, lacks that mind through which he might engage his enemy less violently, with the sweet light of reason, the head and heart in concert. (On this point, it is well to remember how changed the conditions of response since Tate's essay, through the work of the Fugitives and by Weaver, Voegelin, Maritain, Eliade, Niemeyer, and others.) Since the Southerner, which term we enlarge beyond geographic limits, since the "Southerner" lacks that mind, since his "religious conviction is inchoate and unorganized," his one course appears to be a cutting return to roots, rather than merely the spectacle of a rearrangement of the foliage. We spoke earlier of the interesting coincidence of the liberal intellectual's interest in Haley's *Roots,* involving a misunderstanding of the radical action summoned, and Mr. Tate's metaphor speaks to this confusion. Liberalism's "radical" inclinations are as a rule exhibited in some rearrangement of foliage; otherwise the intellectual who is given to radical chic would be forced to explore his own grounding in a most disturbing way. He would have to digest "soul food," not use it as metaphor. That is the root of the comedy in Tom Wolfe's *Radical Chic and Mau-Mauing the Flak Catchers.*

It is most difficult, in so literally violent an age as ours, to talk of violent action without being misunderstood as encouraging the use of bombs and other terroristic instruments. What I am talking about, as I trust is clear, is a radical engagement of existence which we have seen as Flannery O'Connor's concern. The title alone of her second novel is most telling on the point, *The Violent Bear It Away.* The full text from Matthew 11:12 reads, "From the days of John the Baptist until now, the Kingdom of Heaven suffereth violence, and the violent bear it away." Without dwelling upon the multiple meaning of *violence* in the biblical text, we may note that the most deeply significant violence in the novel itself is that whereby the protagonist, young Tarwater, dies to the old man he has been and is born into the new man. It is after this necessarily violent encounter of an individual soul with its own reality that it is at last prepared to enter community; Tarwater embarks in the final scene upon his mission to "WARN THE CHILDREN OF GOD OF THE TERRIBLE SPEED OF MERCY." I should like to show through another fiction than Miss O'Connor's, through a story published the same year as Tate's essay in *I'll Take My Stand,* something of what I mean, though the limits of my public readings mitigate against it. In compromise, I shall request the indulgence of an "Afterword" to be included with the printed version, in which I shall continue to speak to you in community, I dare hope. The story I choose involves violence. It is, in fact, something of a murder mystery involving betrayal in love. But the mystery attaches more to the soul of community than to the violence done to a single man who happens to come into that community and willfully violate it by a seduction. The most significant violations, however, are those of the soul, violations not to be brought to just account without some recognition of the terror of mercy itself, and that recognition must be acknowledged even by the violated. For love is the inclusive climate of the story, a love larger than the presence of Eros. We shall need to remember, as we proceed to our "Afterword," the point made by Andrew Lytle: the opposite of love is not hate, but power. And in connection with this point, we remember as well that the interests of power are as various as the sins of revolt against love, a revolt whose spring is pride. How difficult, given the complication of our attempts upon fully becoming by the constancy of pride in us—how difficult to reconcile the terror of mercy and the righteousness of justice. When next we meet in the "Afterword," I shall first prepare our interest in the story by reflecting on the enigmatic relation of justice and mercy, that most ancient of problems to community, and then look closely at William Faulkner's "A Rose for Emily."

Afterword

A PARTICULAR CONSEQUENCE of the dissociation of the soul's faculties, as that dissociation affects community, is our loss of understanding about the relation of justice to mercy in the affairs of community, for both the virtues of justice and of mercy have been appropriated and secularized through the general gnostic tenor of the times. That is why Miss O'Connor's Rayber, for instance, can believe it a mercy to murder that mistake of nature, his ward Bishop. The ancient enigma of justice's relation to mercy we have been able to set aside without riddling or attempting to riddle it, though we may still "read" Job or *Oedipus Rex* or *The Divine Comedy* or *Paradise Lost.* Those works do not signify mystery for us, for we have, through the academy's ignoring the "ninth part of speech," reduced prophetic poetry to merely poetry. Myth and symbol have been reduced to fiction, in whose name we are inclined to accept poetry, but only as the play of fancy on reality and of no visionary authority. We take literature seriously in one sense: it may be explored as projections of a mind, as psychological specimens, our age's substitute for the somewhat older simplification of literature whereby the poem was a piece of biographical information. We are the less troubled, therefore, when we act in community by reductions of virtue, since they are of a "literary" or "psychological" secular level; mercy may be seen as the just action of correcting a mistake of nature, for instance, as Miss O'Connor's Rayber argues in rationalizing the murder of Bishop.

But as members one of another, in true community, we can neither substitute one secularized virtue for another nor avoid engaging complexities where virtues touch each other. We may not cease from a concern for both justice and mercy. And our engagement of those active virtues requires of us awe and trembling in their exercise. When we operate as autonomous man (in Solzhenitsyn's description of modernism) without a continuing sense of the "inviolable whole" of existence (in Tate's description of our proper deportment), we have lost the recognition of our finitude, the first knowledge necessary to a vision of reality. That we have largely lost sight of the whole horse is reflected in the public broils waged in the name of justice or of mercy over current questions of abortion or capital punishment. Eliot cautions us about the importance of a sense of our finitude in relation to our actions, about the pending finality in each moment. In *Little Gidding,* he reminds us that any action, of words no less than of our gestures in nature,

> Is a step to the block, to the fire, down the sea's throat
> Or to an illegible stone: and that is where we start.
> We die with the dying.

When we have lost the sense of finitude, we conclude ourselves the absolute. We define life and take it or grant it as if we were its creators, as if the finality of either justice or mercy were our own dispensation. By calling mercy justice or justice mercy, we obscure, by nominalist presumptions, the reality those terms approach, as if thereby to solve a dilemma of incompatibles.

It is not that justice and mercy are incompatible, but that we must struggle to understand just how they may touch each other. The problem is that they are, insofar as our limited knowing and understanding of them in time, incommensurate. Justice as a virtue is more immediate to us. It is older in our intellectual history than mercy, although the Old Testament is full of pleas for mercy. And there is a wistful longing for mercy, even in Greek tragedy. To *plead for* and to *accept* are not the same, however. Justice is available to the *ratio;* but it is through the *intellectus* that we approach mercy. Justice can be rationalized, in an older and acceptable sense of that term. Mercy, which we know as a reality and on occasion practice ourselves—always with a gnawing fear—operates in a realm and out of a realm that is somehow "beyond." Its true country is that region toward which we press with the energy of our finitude and under the banner of justice. But when we enter upon the outskirts of the new country, we shall discover that what is our justice dissolves in what is now the region of Love. We hold as a necessary posit that God is just, which means that we define God within the limits of our knowledge. It is a pitiable necessity of our finitude.

I do not, needless to say, suggest that we either can or should abandon the virtue of justice in favor of mercy, which in its secularized extensions has largely destroyed order, its flag emblazoned at last with "anything goes." That is the route we take in attempting instant salvation—as if by accepting all we become the saviors of all creation. What I do mean is that we are, by our fallen finitude, stuck with the enigma of justice in relation to mercy, believing that we deal with a paradox and not a contradiction. When that time of belief comes for each individually, we each have reached a border of time. There we are required to surrender justice to a terror beyond our control, beyond our own will to order that is our guide in time and nature. We are brought to surrender justice and open ourselves to mercy, which is at last perceived as more terrifying than justice in that country of Love. The face of Love we touch, indirectly, through mercy. That is, in the virtue of mercy as a concept to the *ratio,* we sense through *intellectus* the hidden presence of Love in creation. At the outer reaches of our pursuit, the necessary surrender of our finitude burns away the justice-mercy dilemma in the fire of Love. That moment is in a present *beyondness* that returns our selves (my-self) renewed. In such visionary moments we glimpse the incommensurate relation of a time-stained justice and a mystery-stained mercy, rather than their seeming antithesis. We are, in consequence, not left with our soul selves in the same way Keats feels left at the end of his encounter with the nightingale, though our soul self means thenceforth more than it could otherwise mean. In that experience of a still point, of a spot of time, we are enabled to pray that we be taught to care and not to care, that we may sit still in assurance of the fullest action of Love, neither willfully worldly nor otherworldly, but content with the present moment which hints the abiding. That content is one purchased for us in the wild act beyond all our sense of order, beyond any articulation of the commensurate, by that Love that pierces being in time: the Incarnation, the supreme violence that takes and holds the Kingdom of Heaven.

If we cannot quite reach that borderland, we may have intimations of it, as I think William Faulkner does. It is a recognition implicit in that scene in "The Bear" in which the two McCaslins (Ike and Cass Edmonds) walk across bear rugs, with Cass quoting and talking about Keats's pursuit of Beauty in his urn, trying to convince Ike of the necessity of action in the world which does not necessarily deny the larger context. At that point, Ike McCaslin is himself surrendering the world, but it is a partial surrender. He has learned the "not to care" side of the mystery, but not the caring side. He is, as I have argued elsewhere, a passive gnostic who would through his own sacrifice transgress upon Christ's sacrifice with a blindness that leaves him a pathetic, not a tragic, soul. (Ike's recognition of the transgression comes in "Delta Autumn.") Faulkner, I believe, by his heart recognizes the complex country involved, though his head never quite lets him surrender fully to that complexity. The next best possibility, he seems to think, is his commitment to his art, but it is a commitment as artist within which stirs the prophetic, and he does not deny that presence. I think we may discover his epiphany as artist, his moment of grace, in that arresting story, the first major story in his career, in which the prophetic voice discovers its own potential, not for revelation but for affirming the complex mystery of existence as discovered in community. I mean the story "A Rose for Emily," published the same year as *I'll Take My Stand.*

Let us approach our concern by first distinguishing epiphany as it becomes a critical term in our reading of modern literature after Joyce's emphasis upon it and as it is understood by Flannery O'Connor. I do so, anticipating that Faulkner's sense of epiphany falls in between the two. For Joyce, epiphany has limits very like those the young Eliot gives to myth in his discussion of *Ulysses.* That is, as Eliot's term is limited historically in relation to the course of Western poetry and not seen till later to have spiritual grounds, Joyce's term is understood as limited to the individual character's experience of the world, a species of the historical; it is limited to consciousness and is anchored in psychological responses of a character to experience. Joyce does not, I believe, ever come to an enlargement of his sense of epiphany, a term he takes from his theological training but reduces to the uses of a fiction. He never quite pursues epiphany into the mystery of the soul in its response to the created world, a hesitation which leads him to wonder late in his career whether the whole of his work is not itself a creation of fancy rather than of the imagination.

Flannery O'Connor, on the other hand, is quite confident that the whole of reality touches a part of it, and for her this means even that part of reality we call art; the secondary creations of minds are touched by the fullness of reality. That is why she can say with confidence that even the naturalist, insofar as he is true to what he sees in relation to what he makes, will have made more largely than he may himself understand. Thus, she accepts the historical—the particularity of individuals and community in time—as the starting point of art, ignoring neither the latest science nor the oldest history. Her confidence is that through the whole complex of such matter for fiction—insofar as she has practiced an "incarnational" art, anchoring art in reality—mystery will be present. And wherever there is the presence of mystery, there is possible a present operation of the mystery of grace, which we have said earlier is the principal antagonist to her characters. Faulkner, we remember from interviews, may talk of his characters as if they were real, speculating on their careers separate from the fiction that contains them. Flannery O'Connor does so as well. And when she says that she has confidence in the possibility that the grandmother's gesture in "A Good Man Is Hard to Find" has planted mustard seed in the Misfit's heart which may grow to the great crow-filled tree of a Misfit as prophet, she is sharing with Faulkner this sense of a certain actuality in her characters. But there is a difference. Faulkner is always more fully aware of himself as maker of his characters than O'Connor. She has intimations of herself as medium through her gift (though she is insistent on her responsibilities as maker). Here, then, the imitation of the actions of grace in nature, such as that in the story of the Misfit, touches a reality of grace in nature not to be denied; we notice that she manages this openness of her craft largely because she does not allow herself to become entrapped in the problem of justice's relation to mercy. She does not, in consequence, become victim of sentimentality in pursuit of mercy nor a tract writer out of gnostic presumption. One never "proves" anything with a story, she says. It does not follow, however, that a story may not be in itself a form of revelation.

Faulkner, then, comes very near to O'Connor's understanding of the prophetic role of the poet, though much of Faulkner criticism is spent pursuing his concern for justice and mercy, often faulting him for no clear announcement of his position on the dilemma. I propose to use a single critical work, a comment on "A Rose for Emily," to stand for this general critical misdirection, two passages from Dorothy Tuck's *Handbook of Faulkner* (1964):

> Driven from the world of the living by her acts, Miss Emily had only the dead to turn to. But the dead have no pity, and the townsfolk—with the reader—feel only horror at the discovery of murder so deliberately perpetrated and concealed, and a further horror at the suggestion of necrophilia. (P. 175)

> The chief irony in the story lies in the contrast between the townspeople's envious attitude toward Miss Emily and the profound misery of her actual condition. (P. 175)

I think we shall find the story far richer and more complex than this critical summary suggests. The disparity is unfortunate, since the *Handbook* is aimed at young instructors and students for purposes no doubt of term papers and essay exams and so corrupts by simplification. It is clear from the story, for instance, that the townspeople's response to Miss Emily is extremely complex, and that she herself is not simply victim of a "profound misery," given her "actual condition." As Cleanth Brooks has pointed out, the images we have of Miss Emily, and the suggestions made through metaphor, are important. The narrator notes her "cold, haughty black eyes" in a face whose flesh is "strained across the temples," giving her a look such as "you imagine a lighthouse-keeper's face ought to look." Brooks observes that "the keeper of light . . . looks out into darkness. He serves others but lives in sheer isolation himself." The observation leads Mr. Brooks to suggest that for readers who demand a moral, "Miss Emily's story constitutes a warning against the sin of pride: heroic isolation pushed too far ends in homicidal madness."[1] Professor Tuck's reading would have Miss Emily a sort of Richard Cory, when she is more nearly comparable to the woman in A. E. Robinson's "Eros Tyrannos," though the love which Faulkner's story explores is not so simple as the surface attention to Eros in Robinson's poem.

There is often critical applause for the mastery of point of view in this first publication by Faulkner, a praise of his technical skill which is well deserved. But the skillfulness of the telling reaches beyond the merely technical, as an exploration of the similar techniques in the story and in Robinson's poem would reveal. Here we pause only to observe that in Robinson's poem, the dramatic tension lies in the narrator of the poem, suspended between appearances and the uncertainty of appearance as a guide to reality, leaving the voice of the poem suspended in futile balance. Faulkner's narrator is an active agent in the story through whom Faulkner has found a way of entering into the complexity of community, a complexity greater than the surface elements of Miss Emily's mad love or the simple dimensions of law or sociology. Law we assign—or used to assign—responsibility for communal justice; sociology has, meanwhile, largely usurped theology's authority in the mystery of mercy and confused civil order in consequence. In such a topsy-turvy world, it is the prophetic poet who may return us to a clearer perspective upon the complexity of mercy's relation to communal justice, and I believe that to be one of the effects achieved by Faulkner through his point of view.

Let us take a direction into the story beyond the usual—beyond Professor Tuck's and somewhat separate from Mr. Brooks's though touching his observations. Let us consider this an initiation story, with the narrator more central than Miss Emily. I do not believe we may conclude with Professor Tuck that Miss Emily is simply profoundly miserable; certainly, the narrator does not. And I believe as well that a moral informs the story beyond Miss Emily's presence in community as a warning against the sin of pride. Or, let us rather say that instead of a moral out of the particulars of the lives involved, we have rather more interestingly a lesson given us, a dramatization of the answer to the question Tate raises in his essay the year the story appeared. Tate, remember, asks: "How may the Southerner take hold of his Tradition?" I propose the story as an answer to that question, an answer not directly proposed by Faulkner as a response to the explicit question but a discovery he makes in the practice of his art.

We may begin by observing the narrator's summary of Miss Emily's life, which is also a summary of the complex response of the community to Miss Emily. For the townsfolk, "she passed from generation to generation—dear, inescapable, tranquil, and perverse." That understanding of her complexity is the "lesson" learned by our narrator through his tribute to her, a tribute signalled by the title. For the title itself indicates the story to be a votive offering. It is an offering made by an imaginative reliving of community, generation to generation, with Miss Emily a point of time's measure. The narrator also relives responses within particular generations, counterpointing individual responses through an imaginative acceptance and sharing of the particular view of Miss Emily held by particular citizens at particular times. There is a considerable variety in so brief a compass: from the older generation, Colonal Sartoris and Emily's father (who stands over her life and her final death in that crayon portrait, much as Axel Heyst's "fine detachment" is brooded over by the oil portrait of his father that haunts the action in Conrad's *Victory*). There is the minister and his wife, the blood-kin cousins from Alabama (outsiders to the community). The story is thick with graybeards, old women, the young. But more than passing time is signified by counterpointing new generation to old. More than a sense of fiction's duration is at work here; more than art's suggestion of lapsed time. Miss Emily, now dead, "had been a tradition, a duty, a care; a sort of hereditary obligation upon the town." *Upon* the town, whether it wills it or notices it or not.

And it is the younger generation that shies from acknowledging its inheritance, the new generation with its "more modern ideas." We miss a point here to suppose the narrator means only *one* of the generations of this community associated with Miss Emily: it is the "next," successively, Miss Emily a constant presence where complexities are gradually revealed. The inclination to "modern ideas" is a constant in the affairs of a community from generation to generation, which is why Miss Emily is so important a constant to community. That is the narrator's discovery, touched upon as he observes the old men talking on the porch and in the yard while Miss Emily lies in state, receiving the whole town. They are "the very old men" and they talk of her "as if she had been a contemporary of theirs, believing that they had danced with her and courted her perhaps." What we know is that she is younger than they, that in this moment of centering attention, the community is caught up in a recognition of human finitude beyond what they may articulate, dependent as community must be upon the prophetic poet. Finitude is pervasive of community, generation to generation, and it is signalled by old men's dreams of a youth that never was; by "the ladies sibilant and macabre" in their reductionists' attentions to Emily Grierson, deceased; by the young men's captivity to "more modern ideas." And there is an appropriateness to that civil issue that has bound the official town and Miss Emily, the matter of property tax, that tax which more than any other necessity of community since the days of Joseph and Mary tends to reduce justice to the convenient by abstraction, given as it is to a justice generalized. This generalization of the measure of the particular means inevitably a reduction of the person to the demands of the common weal, the common weal so often the point of focus for "more modern ideas." In the story, given such possible discovery, one is almost tempted to suggest that our narrator moves from civil to prophetic service; and there is one hint of evidence to support this suggestion.

If, as I suggest, the story has rich implications when seen as the education of its narrator, we might even conclude that he, by the action of his tribute, becomes not only the consciousness of the community, expressing it, but its conscience as well. He comes to treasure Miss Emily beyond her obvious reduced station in community, a reclusive citizen owing taxes; he also values her, even after he knows that she is not simply peculiar, but mad and not only mad but a murderer, though it may be that the madness follows her murdering Homer Barron, her betrayer, rather than precedes it. (On this theme of madness in relation to love, we may remember Miss O'Connor's Rayber.) Her madness, in relation to the murder she commits, is ambiguously presented; the community participates in the deed more than it will openly acknowledge. For it seems insufficient to that scene with the druggist to conclude that he is ignorant of what is going on when she demands arsenic, or that he gives Miss Emily the poison because of her intimidating presence, or that the town does not share in the plot through the druggist. The community participates at the level of fancy, through a righteousness whose justification is its reflexive concern for justice. (Faulkner's skill is apparent in making it possible for the townsfolk to know and not know: he has Homer appear once more, after Miss Emily purchases the arsenic; Homer having left town once and returned, it may be easily supposed that he has now left for good, as indeed he has. But seeing Homer after the purchase soothes the discomfort over Miss Emily's purchase.)

Our narrator quite clearly associates himself at various points with segments of the community and shares the separate feelings about Miss Emily. She is an object allowing unseemly responses. She arouses anger, envy, self-righteousness, pity, all taken singly being incommensurate responses; but most especially, I suggest the focusing of pity upon Miss Emily is a sign of the community's inadequate response. What is missing in the "account" of Miss Emily, though restored by our narrator, is love. And so we are recalled once more to the title. There is gratitude, a thankfulness, in the narrator for Miss Emily; for it is she and the townsfolk's response to her that lead the narrator to appreciate the complexity of community existence, the intricate way in which we are members one of another. He had lived out the several responses of community, but there is at least a suggestion that our narrator, so concretely present, is initially one of the "new generation." He recounts the visitation of the town fathers upon Miss Emily at midnight with the lime to be scattered, an attempt to blot out the stink of human depravity, as it were. There were in the party "three graybeards and one younger man, a member of the rising generation," who no doubt would have been most insistent to the Board of Aldermen that Miss Emily pay her just portion of city taxes.

The conclusion of the story, with its graphic details so richly put that one smells the ancient dust in the house, is a most effective ending, though it is so immediate to us that we tend to overlook the implications. We may miss the point, for instance, that the townsfolk are still very actively pitiable and superior toward Miss Emily, not to say curious. That room they must have open, not so much to air out the place so that Miss Emily's blood-kin may sell it as to satisfy their sense of mystery. I think a Donne or a Webster would very much appreciate the macabre details as commentary on our common human condition, strengths, and weaknesses. As for our day, we tend rather to be fascinated by, in Professor Tuck's phrase, "a further horror at the suggestion of necrophilia." That is the sort of explanation of the mystery of Miss Emily that keeps epiphany at the psychological level. I suggest a more likely truth about the necrophilia, one I believe the narrator himself is conscious of. We will have noticed the very careful preparation of details concerning Miss Emily's hair. She grows old and her hair, once cut short at the time of her fall, changes. At last it reaches a balance in "an even pepper-and-salt iron-gray" which it continued to hold up till her death at seventy-four, a "vigorous iron-gray, like the hair of an active man." Of course, the townsfolk, save the narrator, have little sense of Miss Emily as vigorous and active. It is such a hair that is lifted from "the second pillow" with its "indention of a head." With "that faint and invisible dust dry and acrid in the nostrils, we saw a long strand of iron-gray hair." Now the "horror . . . of necrophilia" might be significant symbolically to a Dante. But a suspicion of literal necrophilia in Miss Emily's relation to Homer Barron makes little sense at all, given the description of what remains of Homer. "What was left of him . . . had become inextricable from the bed in which he lay; and upon him and upon the pillow beside him lay the even coating of the patient and abiding dust." There has been no suggestion of a second visit to the druggist for preservatives. I suppose as more probable a suggestion of expiation on Miss Emily's part in these concluding sentences. As expiation it lacks the spectacle of Hazel Motes's barbwire around his chest and his self-blinding acts, which we also have difficulty understanding except as psychological aberration. That the dust has long since covered the second pillow might suggest Miss Emily's second stage of expiation, her having moved into the bedroom downstairs and tentatively returned to community through those art lessons. The pillow under her head is "yellow and moldy with age" when she at last dies and the rooms no less dusty than those upstairs. There is a further comment on the townsfolk in closing:

> [Miss Emily's female cousins from Alabama] held the funeral on the second day, with the town coming back to look at Miss Emily beneath a mass of bought flowers, with the crayon face of her father musing profoundly above the bier and the ladies sibilant and macabre; and the very old men . . . on the porch and the lawn, talking of Miss Emily as if she had been a contemporary of theirs.

And our narrator, younger than these, seeing the parts in relation, even appreciating the old men's confused sense of time, "to whom all the past is not a diminishing road but, instead, a huge meadow which no winter ever quite touches, divided from them now by the narrow bottle-neck of the most recent decade of years."

That is the penultimate discovery; the ultimate touches Miss Emily at the deepest point of her particular, personal encounter with the complexity of life in nature and community; he sees the iron-gray hair lifted from the pillow. He is at last prepared to pay tribute to Miss Emily, seeing her as a person "dear, inescapable, impervious, tranquil, and perverse"—a suitable enough characterization of any individual in any real community. He can as well see beyond the bottleneck of the most recent decade or decades, and with a prophetic voice echoing known but forgotten things discovered through Miss Emily tell us with authority that she is to community, in all the strengths and weaknesses those members share with her, "a tradition, a duty, and a care; a sort of hereditary obligation upon the town, dating from that day . . . when Colonel Sartoris . . . remitted her taxes." His act was not an act of civic charity but of communal love, through which she became, given her fallen humanity raised to public focus, an inescapable center of community awareness. She ties past, present, and future. For a community is more likely to be held together by a Miss Emily than by, say, a replica of the Parthenon.

Even so, Faulkner's narrator has not been overwhelmed by such a vision as Mrs. Turpin has in Flannery O'Connor's "Revelation." Mrs. Turpin sees "companies of white-trash, clean for the first time in their lives, and bands of black niggers in white robes, and battalions of freaks and lunatics shouting and clapping and leaping like frogs," with herself and her husband bringing up the rear, those with "a little of everything and the God-given wit to use it right." She and Claude are such because they had always stood for "good order and common sense and respectable behavior." Mrs. Turpin has a glimpse into that country where mercy consumes justice, and she senses at least that in that passage beyond time "even their virtues were being burned away." Such is the experience for her that the darkening path she follows from her modern pigpen to her and Claude's house is lightened by the cricket choruses, the "voices of souls climbing upward into the starry field and shouting hallelujah." Through a violence of activity centering in Mrs. Turpin's mind, particularly in her last-ditch revolt against the reality of her condition as one of God's creation and not the special creature she thinks herself, Miss O'Connor raises our expectations beyond the natural or social levels of existence. Faulkner in his "Rose for Emily," however, advances his narrator only to the social level, though that is a level considerably beyond the analytical measures of community by sociology. His narrator comes to accept, in community, that variety of creatures Mrs. Turpin is shocked by, those who move toward fulfillment ahead of her. He knows freaks, scoundrels, the mad, the hypocritical and pious, the bigoted—in short, God's plenty in a small temporal sphere. And he recognizes community's responsibility beyond the sentimentalized version of Sparta that so largely dominates our day's concern for community through a variety of programs imposed upon it in the name of mercy and with a pretense of justice—and imposed from the top.

In other words, Faulkner's narrator knows, with Davidson and the Agrarians, that "life should determine economics," lest in reversing the two we should threaten "the very existence of human society." We do not need Voegelin's terminology, his analysis of modern gnosticism, to see its presence in Faulkner's community, in each "new generation." Nor do we need Solzhenitsyn's warning of a spirit loosed on the West since the Renaissance, "the proclaimed and enforced autonomy of man from any higher source above him." Within that liberation, the mystery of mercy may be denied in affirming the letter of the law as the supreme arbiter of order in nature, commanded by autonomous man. Faulkner's narrator, let us say, discovers that awesome responsibility that always hovers over the exercise of power in any community which shares assumptions about man's relation to nature and to his fellows. The prophetic poet brings us back toward that condition of spirit in community, though such allies as Voegelin, the philosopher, are most welcomed in their reassurances that we must hold such concerns. We must hold them not because we are a remote, vestigial remnant in nature, as we are considered to be by those born Yankees of the race of man. Certainly we are not a residue of history haunting only the literal Southeast, given to possum hunts and mint juleps, to the oppression of blacks and an artificiality of manners as a cover for the darker self some readers think they find in such Southerners as Miss Emily. The "Southerner" we have pursued is Mr. Tate's regionalist; the "Southernness" we have hoped to rescue is intricate to place always. But it is so because of that universal presence in place which Voegelin describes as the condition of existence in reality, that one "constant in the history of mankind" reflected in the "language of tension" between self-love and the love of God, between an openness of spirit and its closure against being, between truth and untruth, life and death—to deny which poles is to obscure the reality of existence. It does not in spite of our attempts to the contrary destroy that reality. And that is the reassuring principle so richly argued by that "Southerner" upon whom I have depended for support of the *ratio*'s case for "Southernness," St. Thomas Aquinas, even as the *intellectus*'s testimony on a universal "Southernness" is dramatized for us by St. Augustine.

Notes

Preface

1. In his "Preface" to *The Anathemata,* Jones says: "I mean by my title as much as it can be made to mean, or can evoke or suggest, however obliquely: the blessed things that have taken on what is cursed and the profane things that somehow are redeemed: the delights and also the 'ornaments,' both in the primary sense of gear and paraphernalia and in the sense of what simply adorns; the donated and votive things, the things dedicated after whatever fashion, the things in some sense made separate by being 'laid up from other things'; things, or some aspect of them, that partake of the extra-utile and of the gratuitous; things that are the signs of something other, together with those signs that not only have the nature of a sign, but are themselves, under some mode, what they signify. Things set up, lifted up, or in whatever manner made over to the gods." The passage sheds a particular light on Allen Tate's forlorn, very modern speaker in "Ode to the Confederate Dead," a commemoration from the living who have lost an understanding of the act of commemoration which is the lifting up of sacred and profane things, both of which are, for Jones, sacred.

> What shall we say who have knowledge
> Carried to the heart? Shall we take the act
> To the grave? Shall we, more hopeful, set up the grave
> In the house? The ravenous grave?

2. Perhaps because the Latin classics were so pervasive in our formal life before 1865—reflected in names no less than definitions of institutions—we have tended to overlook the strong Northman aspect in the Southern tradition. Its presence is rather conspicuous in actions and events of that old war itself, though I leave it to someone else to develop the theme more fully. Here I only remark the *comitatus* mode reflected in the deportment of local volunteer groups, especially in the opening stages

of the War Between the States. It is a commonplace observation of the relation of thane to lord in the old sagas: a commitment to blood ties which in parts of the South extended into community to the point that all were more nearly a people more particular than race, almost at the level of family. The "election" of officers within volunteer groups partakes of this Northern European heroic tradition, the pressure of emergency accelerating the elevation of a "lord," whereas in the older tradition he emerged more slowly. If it was sometimes a matter of social position at the beginning of the war that led to elevation, it was accompanied with the expectation that the leader would live up to that older code through his bravery, honor, devotion to a cause. To understand this presence in the Southern disposition helps explain the veneration in which Lee was and (though to a lesser degree) still is held. But it will especially enlighten his soldiers' devotion to Stonewall Jackson, especially in the Shenandoah Valley Campaign. The lingering ambience of that campaign is as important a touchstone to historical consciousness in some minds as any other aspect of the conflict. It helps explain, among other things, the young Fugitive poets' interest in Jackson and Forrest in biographies. The tragic mood of Davidson's Lee in "Lee in the Mountains" suggests in Davidson himself a recognition of a difference between the reflective, intellectual stoicism of a Lee and the active engagement of Fate by a Jackson or Forrest.

The point is of such importance that I must turn to a surviving symbol of this North European heritage as separate from our Mediterranean heritage. In the cemetery on Prospect Hill at Front Royal, Virginia, are buried thirty or forty of Colonel Mosby's men. They lie within a circular iron fence that separates the outer world. But they are circled about a central memorial shaft of marble declaring them "Mosby's Men." The headstones face outward, with individual names and dates on which they were killed in action. The spectator's impression is of a last stand, as if at the Battle of Maldon when the Anglo-Saxons stood against the Viking invaders. Nearby, there is another monument, also raised by surviving Mosby Men, but quite different in symbolic tenor. It stands bare and open, an indictment of a treacherous enemy rather than a celebration of a community of warriors held by *comitatus* honor. Here are remembered those soldiers and random civilians summarily executed by Sheridan on suspicion of their being Mosby Men. On this monument is the more traditional Roman address from Horace: "Dulce et decorum est pro patria mori." The monument is flanked incongruously by two ship's cannons. The distance between the two monuments is a few paces on the hillside. But they are almost two civilizations apart in one sense, reminding us of the complexities in our Old World heritage.

There is a fatalistic presence in that North European tradition, as in the Roman, which anticipates the defeat even of the gods themselves by evil. But beyond the Virgilian mode of lament for the "tears of things," there is in this tradition the heroic recklessness of uncompromising resistance. The honorable man by his honor is destined to death against the unacceptable. In the Fugitive-Agrarians, I suspect, there is a constant tension between the poles suggested here—between the lessons of *Beowulf* on the one hand and of *The Aeneid* on the other, which tension is crucial to the reading of Davidson's and Tate's poetry. This thread of the North European heroic in us might also help explain the deportment of a defeated people under a vindictive conqueror in the years immediately after 1865. One might show that Faulkner, among our Southern writers, is deeply aware of this thread in our heritage, dramatized in John Sartoris and Sutpen among others, and in relation to that Faulknerian theme, the conflict between the heroics of merely enduring and the heroics of prevailing. On the point in general, see E. V. Gordon's introductory discussion of "The Heroic Literature of the North," in his *Introduction to Old Norse,* in relation to Allen Tate's *Stonewall Jackson: The Good Soldier* and Holmes A. Alexander's *Washington and Lee: A Study in the Will to Win.*

3. I am quite deliberately enlarging the term *fundamentalism,* intending to rescue it if I may from its merely pejorative associations. Biblical scholarship in the nineteenth century, aside from valuable textual discoveries, managed to introduce darkness as well as light, becoming increasingly allied with that scientific spirit which seemed intent upon rationalizing all things. It had the effect largely of anthropomorphizing Christianity from within. By the turn of the century, textual scholars seemed ranged on the side of Darwin. The immediate response of the Fundamentalist was to save scripture by embracing it literally. There have been since those days highly visible, comically extreme defenders of the letter of scripture whose absurdities make them quotable for purposes of caricature. The temptation to caricature, by some detractors, is necessary in order to obscure valid ground that lies behind the reaction. Those antagonists of a fundamentalism more deeply based than desperation have quite a different task when the "fundamentalist" is a St. Augustine or St. Thomas or a Gilson or Voegelin or Richard Weaver. When the spirit is removed from the letter by hostile explication, one may in angry panic cling to the letter. What I suggest, however, is that one may discover, if one looks closely, that the armies thus pitted are largely ignorant on both sides: literalist believers in science against literalist believers in scripture. The religious Fundamentalist, out of the shocked sense of being robbed but without a sound intellectual preparation and history of and training

in exegesis that might choose more solid ground, seems easily routed. There is a popular version of the engagement in the famous Scopes Trial, generally taken by the popular intellectual spirit as a test of the benighted by the enlightened. If one consider carefully Richard Weaver's "Dialectic and Rhetoric at Dayton, Tennessee" in *The Ethics of Rhetoric,* one must adjust the popular version of that trial. One regrets that Protestant Fundamentalists in general have forgotten the support given them by St. Augustine in his mastery of an exegesis which does not sacrifice spirit to letter.

4. On this general point, see Stanley L. Jaki's Gifford Lectures, *The Road of Science and the Ways to God;* Etienne Gilson, *From Aristotle to Darwin and Back Again: A Journey in Final Causality, Species, and Evolution;* Eric Voegelin, *The New Science of Politics* and *Science, Politics, and Gnosticism;* Frederick Crews, "The Freudian Way of Knowledge," *The New Criterion* (June 1984); Richard John Neuhaus, "What the Fundamentalists Want," *Commentary* (May 1985).

ONE
First, Catch a Possum

1. I myself would not be surprised to discover that there is already written a top secret report from the first moon landing that says a possum was discovered on the moon, staring in at a porthole, when the dust settled—a mystery too disturbing to allow its general dissemination. We carry with us always our lowly origins, the most elementary level of existence, the most fundamental gift of being, with which and against which we struggle, too often in ignorance of the point where struggle must begin. William Faulkner on occasion praises this dogged cussedness of our humanity, as in his "Address to the U.S. National Commission for UNESCO" (Denver, Colorado, October 2, 1959). Khrushchev's threat that communism will bury capitalism, Faulkner says, is right. "That funeral will occur about ten minutes after the police bury gambling. Because simple man . . . will bury them both. . . . The last sound on the worthless earth will be two human beings trying to launch a home-made space ship and already quarreling about where they are going next." And listening to them, perhaps already aboard, our possum.

2. In the summer of 1985 a considerable stir in the media occurred when speech pathologists began an active campaign to restructure Southern speech in an attempt to get rid of regional accent. Students in Atlanta

paid $45 for quick lessons that would de-South their mouth—for reasons most interesting. One woman interested in marketing thought that change a necessity. Another, a computer programmer, found her speech standing in her way as a programmer. A receptionist, when her company moved to a new office, had her courses paid for by her bosses since "they wanted to change the atmosphere" within the new decor. Another credited her winning first runner-up in the Miss National Teenage Pageant to having acquired "Yankeespeak."

3. Barfield concludes his chapter with these summary words: "There is no more striking example than the Darwinian theory of that borrowing from the experimental by the non-experimental sciences. . . . It was found that the appearances on earth so much lack the regularity of the appearances in the sky that no systematic hypothesis will fit them. But astronomy and physics had taught men that the business of science is to find hypotheses to save the appearances. By a hypothesis, then, these earthly appearances must be saved; and saved they were by the hypothesis of—chance variation. Now the concept of chance is precisely what a hypothesis is devised to save us from. Chance, in fact, [equals] no hypothesis. Yet so hypnotic, at this moment in history, was the influence of the idols and of the special mode of thought which had begotten them, that only a few . . . were troubled by the fact that the impressive vocabulary of technological investigation was actually being used to denote its breakdown; as though, because it is something we can do with ourselves in water, drowning should be included as one of the different ways of swimming." I recommended also the chapter "Original Participation," which develops the argument that "Participation is the extra-sensory relation between man and phenomena." I believe Barfield's "participation" is compatible with St. Thomas's "simple knowledge," which I presently introduce. It serves as well some rescue from the dead end of phenomenology that begins with Husserl and ends with Sartre. On this dead end, see my extended argument, *Why Poe Drank Liquor.*

4. A concern for order has been the most constant theme in literary, political, and philosophical pursuits since World War I, a clear evidence of our distintegration; and a division of the seekers can be made between those who believe man can and must, through his own power, establish order and those who believe order must have a larger reference than man himself, this latter a theme of our lectures. We might note a significant difference in the position Ezra Pound takes on the point from Eliot's position. Pound, echoing *The Great Digest,* takes Confucius's side, arguing in Canto XIII, the high point of Kung's teaching:

> If a man have not order within him
> He can not spread order about him;
> And if a man have not order within him
> His family will not act with due order.

The root of order in the *Digest* lies "in sorting things into organic categories," this extension of knowledge to be attained by "precise verbal definitions." All follows from this root. That Eliot senses an eighteenth-century rationalism underlying Pound's position is indicated by his own recasting of Kung's message given in Canto XIII: "If humility and purity be not in the heart, they are not in the home: and if they are not in the home, they are not in the City" (Choruses from *The Rock*). In Canto XIII Pound appropriates a position so near St. Paul's that he finds it necessary to warn that his sense of community as "body" is not St. Paul's. In Romans 12:4ff., Paul, after his metaphor of the individual as member in the body whose head is Christ, admonishes us to be "kindly affectionate one to another with brotherly love; in honour prefering one another." But Pound's Kung "gave the words 'order' / and 'brotherly deference' / And said nothing of the 'life after death,' " as St. Paul does.

5. The point of departure in this summary is St. Thomas's *On Being and Essence,* explored by Gilson in the subsequent writings of St. Thomas. In that initial work, Thomas introduces the "principle of proper proportionality," whereby one gains some glimpse of the mystery of that relation of the created to the Creator. The argument runs (in an oversimplified rendering): Being, the perfection of all perfections, cannot be conceptualized, as can *esse.* It is approached after conceptualization of *esse* occurs by the mind through a movement of mind—an act of judgment, what I suggest is an active assent. In this movement of mind from *esse* toward Being, mind is turned from itself and its own acts of conceptualizations outward to what is not itself and so on toward that which is beyond conceptualization. The distinction of these two movements of mind (conceptualization and judgment) has its cause implicit in the formulation, "God *is esse;* creatures (*ens*) *have esse* but *are not esse.*" Being may thus be recognized as an uncaused action beyond finite conceptualization. Hence it is called "the perfection of all perfections," the perfection whereby *beings* (*ens*) are. St. Augustine in retrospect acts out this movement of mind for us in his "Vision at Ostia" (book 9, Chap. 10 of *The Confessions*). Following him, I suggest we already in a sense "know" this perfection through *intellectus,* as opposed to the knowing of the *ratio,* the conceptualizing agency of mind. That knowledge is already in the infant's clasp of its mother. Here is the movement in the visionary "con-fusion" spoken

of earlier, the moment at which we are returned to known but forgotten things more fundamental than the limits of time and space. St. Augustine explores this movement at length and with wonder in book 10 of *The Confessions,* "A Philosophy of Memory," and in book 11, "Time and Eternity."

6. See Wolfgang Kayser, *The Grotesque in Art and Literature.*

TWO
Possums in the In-Between

1. Timothy McDermott, appendix IIIm, vol. 2 (1a, 2–11), Blackfriars *Summa Theologiae,* p. 182.

2. Ibid., p. 185.

3. Flannery O'Connor, "Some Aspects of the Grotesque in Southern Fiction," in *Mystery and Manners,* pp. 48–49.

4. This is a point developed at length in relation to Hawthorne in my *Why Hawthorne Was Melancholy.*

5. See *Freedom and Economics: A World-Wide Survey of Economic Freedoms Existing Today,* prepared by Citizens Economic Foundation (Houston, Texas, 1984).

6. My realist seems to have a point, given the activist sentimentality so pervasive of our world, though his avoiding the reality of my little possum by declaring it a repugnant creature may be as sentimentalized a response to creation as Mrs. Roosevelt's. Both miss the point of analogy, of metaphor—the one offended by a purported likeness in unlike things, the other through an excess that obscures the significant term *unlike things.* A flock of ducks over the Caribbean is not an equivalent of a Pan Am flight. I have taken no Gallup survey of the relative proportions of possum realists and possum sentimentalists, though I suspect that the latter predominate, especially since direct encounters with possums nationwide are infrequent and our being removed from the proximate cause of sentiment is one of the more promising conditions in the popular spirit for sentimentality to flourish.

7. The tonal presence of sentimentality in a particular person's words is quite various, ranging from acid cynicism to open heart gushing, though tone proceeds from a common mis-taking of creation. If on the one hand one finds a laconic wittiness, on the other there is likely uncontrolled oohing and aahing. But at either extreme, analogy (whether denied or abused) is not the culprit. Analogy is the principal means whereby we touch upon the structure of creation. That is, analogy helps us in the

necessary pursuit of the fundamental ground of being, though poet and philosopher alike are at risk in its use. For Plato, Virgil, and Lucretius, analogy is a calculated risk in the search for order. For John Keats, it appears largely a temptation through the senses to an illusion. For St. Thomas, it is the only way whereby we may move beyond the isolation of our unrealized potential, the most fundamental way, given the gifts of intellect, whereby we may remove obstacles to the operation of grace.

8. William Buckley, in his syndicated column (*Atlanta Journal,* July 15, 1985), reports a solicitation of his support in *Playboy*'s advertising campaign to defend itself against what the solicitor (the magazine's editorial director) calls "a kind of moral terrorism" by boycott and "on-site harassment" by "right-wing groups and—because zealotry makes strange bedfellows—some left-wing groups as well." One notes here the puzzlement that even the left is on occasion offended by the deliberate corrosion of morals practiced by *Playboy.* Buckley comments that "we have traveled a long distance from Nathaniel Hawthorne, who awarded a scarlet letter to adulterers, to Hugh Hefner, who thinks adultery is good plain American wholesome fun and takes pride in his magazine as the principal architect of the sexual revolution."

9. There is, I suggest, one instance in our tradition where the public display of passionate agony was unavoidable and salutary, the Crucifixion. But the two events are incommensurate, not because the one lies in art, the other in history. The Crucifixion occurs at a moment of reconciliation of the whole world to the Cause of the world, though even it is open to and has at times been desecrated by an extreme of sentimentality. It is a moment of high comedy, in Dante's sense of that term, more than of high tragedy as with Oedipus, a distinction worth meditative discourse beyond what we may here allow ourselves.

10. Eliot suggests in "The Metaphysical Poets" (1921) that, following such poets as Jonson and Chapman, whose "mode of feeling was directly and freshly altered by their reading and thought," there occurred a separation of sensibilities. For such poets as Donne, "a thought . . . was a feeling; it modified his sensibility." But in the seventeenth century, "a dissociation of sensibility set in, from which we have never recovered," a separation "aggravated by the influence of the two most powerful poets of the century, Milton and Dryden." One consequence was that "language became more refined, the feeling became more crude." A second effect was the emergence of the "sentimental age," with poets increasingly in revolt "against the ratiocinative. . . . they thought and felt by fits, unbalanced; they reflected." I have taken a longer and wider and (I hope) deeper survey

of this dissociation in *The Reflective Journey toward Order* (1973) and in a study of *The Waste Land, Eliot's Reflective Journey to the Garden* (1979).

11. And so, given such concerns for concrete universals, concerns for the wedding of tame abstracts and wild particulars, we may discover that titles out of such concerns mean more than merely labels. We shall begin here to weave a tapestry of titles given us by poets increasingly moved by the prophetic concern of recalling us to known but forgotten things. *Poems About God,* with the preposition capitalized and raised in importance; "Sweeney among the Nightingales," the preposition hinting our reductions of man in the scale of being. And there is Davidson's own "Lee in the Mountains," ironic prophecy turning on the inconspicuous *in* whose meanings multiply in the poem itself.

12. That these Voegelinean ideas have parallel in the thought of the maturing Fugitives needs only a close reading of the preface to *I'll Take My Stand* to establish, to which one adds the broader scope of *Who Owns America?* And one remembers as well Voegelin's years at Louisiana State University and the lifelong friendships established there with men like Cleanth Brooks and Robert Heilman, friends mutual to the Agrarians and Voegelin.

13. At the same time, I suspect that the spiritual disquiet in Eliot's poem was as disturbing to Williams as the intellectual complexities of the poem that seemed to require academic explication.

THREE
Possum, Posse, Potui

1. Davidson's objections are not the same as those of William Carlos Williams. For Williams, what is required is almost an abandoning of the eight parts of speech in favor of complete immersion in the ninth, an attempt as I have suggested elsewhere to regain by an act of the will the primitive state of soul of a Grandma Moses. While Williams never forgives Eliot for *The Waste Land* (see his *Autobiography*), he nevertheless discovers the importance of the eight parts of speech, as he is increasingly forced to abandon a simple *ad hoc* response to encounters of the world. His *Paterson* is consequently much nearer Davidson's concerns for tradition, and in his later poetry we find him increasingly raising some of those large metaphysical questions.

2. Eric Voegelin, in *Plato and Aristotle* (pp. 138–139), points out that the poet in Plato's *Ion* and the poet of his *Republic* are held suspect in their relation to the *polis;* insofar as they are imitators, mimetic artists, they

remain low in the rank of men's callings to service in the body of the *polis,* the community; they remain low in the scale of office. But in the *Phaedrus,* whose concern is the realm of the human soul, there appears ranked at the top of the hierarchy of souls, along with the *philosophos,* the *philokalos*—the Lover of Beauty. The two terms name modes of the soul in its highest callings to being: as philosopher, the soul seeks the truth of things; as Lover of Beauty it is possessed by the *mania,* the desire for good which gives appetite (as it were, hunger) for wisdom. These Platonic modes of the soul, it seems to me, have sound analogy to those Thomistic modes of the soul we have already argued, the mode of the *ratio* and that of the *intellectus,* the rational and intuitive, the head and the heart. Concerning Plato's elevation of the *philokalos* beside the *philosophos,* Voegelin remarks, "This *philokalos* is the new poet, truly possessed by the *mania.*" What I wish to suggest is that one has here a workable definition of the prophetic poet.

3. That fancy's poetry may be arresting for the moment is clear from the work of Wallace Stevens, for whom "Modern Poetry" is produced by "the mind in the act of finding what will suffice."

4. Sometimes history itself is not local but imported or manufactured. At Fishguard, in Wales, there is a circle of stones echoing Druidic worship recently installed for the benefit of American visitors. And we have our Alpine Village, Helen, Georgia, whose most famous local product is the Cabbage Patch Doll, not long since pirated in Hong Kong. On this point of local color crystallized and processed, we need reminding again of the Fugitives' insistence in the first issue of their magazine. They flee from nothing faster, they say, "than from the high-caste Brahmins of the Old South," though the New England version is even less welcome to them.

5. On the consequences of this control, separate from the spectacles of "monkey trials" or "prayer in the schools," see Professor Warren Leamon's excellent essay, "Who Controls Public Schools?" *Southern Partisan* 5, no. 2 (Spring 1985).

6. A recent feature in the *Atlanta Journal-Constitution* (July 14, 1985) by Tom Eblen, "60 Years Ago, Scopes Trial a Media Circus," is a well-informed news coverage of the myth which makes one hopeful of media recovery.

7. Mr. Tate endorses, by his choice of terms, the traditional structure of the liberal education, derived from classical and scholastic models. There is, for instance, an explicitly named evolution in the mind's train-

ing, moving from grammar to logic to rhetoric. For a lively exploration of this structure and of its pertinence to contemporary education, see Dorothy Sayers's essay, "The Lost Tools of Learning."

8. See the Hoover Institute Press volume, *Solzhenitsyn in Exile* (1985), and Michael Scammell's *Solzhenitsyn: A Biography* (New York: Norton, 1985).

9. The Agrarians were less than enthusiastic about the humanists, their "Statement of Principles" distinguishing genuine humanism from "an abstract moral 'check' derived from the classics—it was not soft material poured in from the top. It was deeply founded in the way of life itself—in its tables, chairs, portraits, festivals, laws, marriage customs. We cannot recover our native humanism by adopting some standard of taste that is critical enough to question the contemporary arts but not critical enough to question the social and economic life that is their ground."

10. Eric Voegelin, who will have much to say of the nature of the individual in relation to community. In his doctoral dissertation, completed the year *The Waste Land* was published, he makes a comparative study of categories in Georg Simmel's and Othmar Spann's sociologies; that is, in Ellis Sandoz's words (*The Voegelinian Revolution,* p. 38), Voegelin examines "the difference between Simmel's individualistic and Spann's universalistic theories of community." The fruition of this concern is *Order and History,* volume 2 of which is *The World of the Polis*. The concern in the volume is with the emergence of "the Hellenic polis with the symbolic form of philosophy," to be seen in relation to and complementary of volume 1, *Israel and Revelation*. The epigraph for volume 2 is significant, from St. Augustine's *De vera religiones:* "In the study of creature, one should not exercise a vain and perishing curiosity, but ascend toward what is immortal and everlasting."

11. An irony worth noting: Voegelin's *The Authoritarian State* sees parallels between the Averroist conception of the *intellectus unus* and the position established by fascist doctrine—the transference of the transcendent to the locus of particular world-immanent minds. The state, thereby, is made a "spiritual power." Voegelin, (in his "Autobiographical Memoir" given to Ellis Sandoz) remembers confronting a colleague on the law faculty at Vienna who had identified Voegelin as a "Jew" for Nazi purposes. Voegelin demanded to know the evidence for such assertion. "Reason? I am quoting: 'Our people are not as intelligent as you are.' " Since Averroes was a Semite, that the ideology of Nazi Germany itself might be "Semitic" was disturb-

ing. Says Voegelin: "certain thinkers like Carl Schmitt seriously doubted that the National Socialist collectivism had anything to do with such dirty Semitic origins" (Sandoz, *The Voegelinian Revolution,* pp. 63–64).

12. Eliade, in *The Forge and the Crucible: The Origins and Structures of Alchemy,* speaks to our point: "We must not believe that the triumph of experimental science reduced to nought the dreams and ideals of the alchemist. . . . the ideology of the new epoch, crystallized around the myth of infinite progress and boosted by the experimental sciences and the progress of industrialization which dominated and inspired the whole of the nineteenth century, takes up and carries forward . . . the millenary dream of the alchemist. It is in the specific dogma of the nineteenth century, according to which man's true mission is to transform and improve upon Nature and become her master, that we must look for the authentic continuation of the alchemist's dream. . . . one cannot help noticing that . . . synthetic products demonstrate for the first time the possibility of eliminating Time and preparing . . . substances which it would have taken Nature thousands of years to produce. . . . On the plane of cultural history . . . the alchemists, in their desire to supersede Time, anticipated what is in fact the essence of the ideology of the modern world. . . . [Alchemy] has left us its faith in the transmutation of Nature and its ambition to control Time."

13. We must then measure progress in this manner: an institution is declared among the top fifty-five in the country in its research accomplishment on the basis of having received x number of millions of dollars for research. Given that criterion, and the level of thought in operation, our academic institutions are hardly a circumstance by comparison to the research contribution of poverty programs, since they receive many times x number of millions of dollars.

14. See the history of the deliberate starvation of seven million Ukrainians during 1931–1934, conveniently ignored in the West until recently. The details are given in Ewald Ammende's *Human Life in Russia* (New York: John T. Zubal, 1985).

Afterword

1. Brooks, *William Faulkner: First Encounters,* p. 14.

Bibliography

THIS BIBLIOGRAPHY, though selective, is intended to record not only those works bearing most immediately upon the lectures, but those that have influenced the climate of heart and mind out of which the lectures were composed. It has not seemed necessary to include reference to some works which seem to me a sufficiently common property with my reader.

Adams, Henry. *The Education of Henry Adams.* New York: Modern Library, 1931.

Alexander, Holmes A. *Washington and Lee: A Study in the Will to Win.* Boston: Western Islands, 1966.

Aquinas, Saint Thomas. *Introduction to St. Thomas Aquinas.* Edited with an introduction by Anton C. Pegis. New York: Modern Library, 1948.

______. *On Being and Essence.* Translated with an introduction and notes by Armand Maurer. Second revised edition. Toronto: Pontifical Institute of Medieval Studies, 1983.

______. *Treatise on the Virtues.* Translated by John A. Oesterle. Questions 49–67 of the *Summa Theologiae.* Notre Dame: University of Notre Dame Press, 1984.

Aries, Philippe. *The Hour of Our Death.* Translated by Helen Weaver. New York: Alfred A. Knopf, 1981.

Augustine, Saint. *City of God.* Translated by Gerald G. Walsh et al. Edited with an introduction by Vernon J. Bourke. New York: Doubleday Image Books, 1958.

______. *The Confessions of St. Augustine.* Translated by John K. Ryan. New York: Doubleday Image Books, 1960.

Barfield, Owen. *Saving the Appearances: A Study in Idolatry.* New York: Harcourt, Brace and World, 1965.

Bradford, M. E. *Remembering Who We Are: Observations of a Southern Conservative.* Athens: University of Georgia Press, 1985.

BIBLIOGRAPHY

Brooks, Cleanth. *William Faulkner: First Encounters.* New Haven: Yale University Press, 1983.

Dame Julian of Norwich. *Revelations of Divine Love.* Edited from the manuscript by Dom Roger Hudleston. London: Burnes Oates, 1927.

Davidson, Donald. *The Attack on Leviathan: Regionalism and Nationalism in the United States.* Chapel Hill: University of North Carolina Press, 1938.

———. *Poems: 1922–1961.* Minneapolis: University of Minnesota Press, 1966.

———. *Southern Writers in the Modern World.* Athens: University of Georgia Press, 1958.

Eliade, Mircea. *The Forge and the Crucible.* New York: Harper and Row, 1971.

———. *Myth and Reality.* New York: Harper and Row, 1963.

———. *Myths, Rites, Symbols: A Mircea Eliade Reader.* Edited by Wendell C. Beane and William G. Doty. Two volumes. New York: Harper Colophon Books, 1975.

Eliot, T. S. *After Strange Gods: A Primer of Modern Heresy.* New York: Harcourt, Brace and Company, 1933.

Fredrickson, George M. *The Inner Civil War: Northern Intellectuals and the Crisis of the Union.* New York: Harper and Row, 1965.

Gilby, Thomas. *Poetic Experience: An Introduction to Thomist Aesthetic.* New York: Sheed and Ward, 1934.

Gilson, Etienne. *From Aristotle to Darwin and Back Again: A Journey in Final Causality, Species, and Evolution.* Translated by John Lyon. Notre Dame: University of Notre Dame Press, 1984.

———. *The Spirit of Thomism.* New York: Harper Torchbooks, 1964.

Gordon, E. V. *An Introduction to Old Norse.* Second edition, revised by A. R. Taylor. Oxford: Clarendon Press, 1966.

Graff, Gerald. *Literature against Itself: Literary Ideas in Modern Society.* Chicago: University of Chicago Press, 1979.

I'll Take My Stand. By Twelve Southerners. New York: Harper and Brothers, 1930.

Jaki, Stanley L. *The Origin of Science and the Science of Its Origin.* South Bend: Regnery Gateway, 1979.

———. *The Road of Science and the Ways to God.* The Gifford Lectures, 1974–75 and 1975–76. Chicago: University of Chicago Press, 1978.

Johnson, Paul. *Modern Times: The World from the Twenties to the Eighties.* New York: Harper and Row, 1983.

Jonas, Hans. *The Gnostic Religion: The Message of the Alien God and the Beginnings of Christianity.* Second revised edition. Boston: Beacon Press, 1963.

Jones, David. *The Anathemata: Fragments of an Attempted Writing.* New York: Viking Press, 1965.

Kayser, Wolfgang. *The Grotesque in Art and Literature.* Translated by Ulrich Weisstein. New York: McGraw-Hill Book Company, 1966.

Lytle, Andrew. *A Wake for the Living: A Family Chronicle.* New York: Crown Publishers, 1975.

Maritain, Jacques. *Art and Scholasticism.* Translated by J. F. Scanlan. New York: Charles Scribner's Sons, n.d.

______. *The Peasant of the Garonne.* Translated by Michael Cuddihy and Elizabeth Hughes. New York: Holt, Rinehart and Winston, 1968.

Mongtomery, Marion. "Bells for John Stewart's *Burden.*" *Georgia Review,* 20, no. 2 (Summer 1966): 145–181.

______. *Eliot's Reflective Journey to the Garden.* Troy, N.Y.: Whitston Publishing Company, 1979.

______. *The Prophetic Poet and the Spirit of the Age.* Three volumes. La Salle: Sherwood Sugden and Company, 1981–84. (Vol. I, *Why Flannery O'Connor Stayed Home,* 1981; Vol. II, *Why Poe Drank Liquor,* 1983; Vol. III, *Why Hawthorne Was Melancholy,* 1984.)

______. *The Reflective Journey toward Order: Essays on Dante, Wordsworth, Eliot, and Others.* Athens: University of Georgia Press, 1973.

______. "Solzhenitsyn as Southerner." In *Why the South Will Survive.* Edited by Clyde Wilson. Athens: University of Georgia Press, 1981.

Niemeyer, Gerhart. *Between Nothingness and Paradise.* Baton Rouge: Louisiana State University Press, 1971.

O'Connor, Flannery. *The Habit of Being: Letters.* Edited with an introduction by Sally Fitzgerald. New York: Farrar, Straus and Giroux, 1979.

______. *Mystery and Manners.* Foreword by Sally and Robert Fitzgerald. New York: Farrar, Straus and Giroux, 1969.

Olson, Steve. *Biotechnology: An Industry Comes of Age.* Washington, D.C.: National Academy Press, 1986.

Percy, William Alexander. *Lanterns on the Levee: Recollections of a Planter's Son.* New York: Alfred A. Knopf, 1941.

Pieper, Josef. *In Tune with the World: A Theory of Festivity.* Chicago: Franciscan Herald Press, 1973.

______. *Leisure: The Basis of Culture.* Introduction by T. S. Eliot. New York: New American Library, 1963.

Ransom, John Crowe. *God without Thunder: An Unorthodox Defense of Orthodoxy.* New York: Harcourt, Brace and Company, 1930.

———. *Poems About God.* New York: Henry Holt and Company, 1919.

Sandoz, Ellis. *The Voegelinian Revolution: A Biographical Introduction.* Baton Rouge: Louisiana State University Press, 1982.

Sartre, Jean-Paul. *The Words.* Translated by Bernard Frechtman. New York: George Braziller, 1964.

Sayers, Dorothy L. "The Lost Tools of Learning." *National Review,* January 19, 1979, pp. 90–95, 98–99.

Solzhenitsyn, Alexander. *From under the Rubble.* Translated under the direction of Michael Scammell. Boston: Little, Brown and Company, 1975.

———. "A World Split Apart." *National Review,* July 7, 1978, pp. 836–841, 855.

Stern, Karl. *The Flight from Woman.* New York: Farrar, Straus and Giroux, 1965.

Tate, Allen. *Essays of Four Decades.* Chicago: Swallow Press, 1968.

———. *Poems.* New York: Charles Scribner's Sons, 1960.

———. *Stonewall Jackson: The Good Soldier.* New York: G. P. Putnam's Sons, 1928.

Tuck, Dorothy. *Crowell's Handbook of Faulkner.* New York: Thomas Y. Crowell Company, 1964.

Voegelin, Eric. *Conversations with Eric Voegelin.* Edited with an introduction by R. Eric O'Connor. Montreal: Thomas More Institute, 1980.

———. *Der Autoritaere Staat.* Vienna: Springer, 1936.

———. *From Enlightenment to Revolution.* Edited by John H. Hallowell. Durham: Duke University Press, 1975.

———. *The New Science of Politics.* Chicago: University of Chicago Press, 1952.

———. *Order and History.* Baton Rouge: Lousiana State University Press, 1956–74. (Vol. I, *Israel and Revelation,* 1956; Vol. II, *The World of the Polis,* 1957; Vol. III, *Plato and Aristotle,* 1957; Vol. IV, *The Ecumenic Age,* 1974.)

———. *Science, Politics, and Gnosticism.* Chicago: Henry Regnery Company, 1968.

Weaver, Richard. *The Ethics of Rhetoric.* Chicago: Henry Regnery Company, 1953.

———. *Ideas Have Consequences.* Chicago: University of Chicago Press, 1948.

———. *The Southern Tradition at Bay: A History of Post-Bellum Thought.* New Rochelle: Arlington House, 1968.

Index